MAKING C

Christian Nurture, Family Worship and Church Growth

MAKING CONTACT

Christian Nurture, Family Worship and Church Growth

LESLIE J. FRANCIS

with Andrew Bowden, John Duckett, David Lankshear,
Katherine Musson, Paddy Phillips, Nicola Slee,
and Doreen Storr

Preface by John M. Hull

COLLINS

Collins Liturgical Publications
8 Grafton Street, London, W1X 3LA

Distributed in Ireland by
Educational Company of Ireland
21 Talbot Street, Dublin 1

Collins Liturgical Australia
P.O. Box 316 Blackburn,Victoria 3130

ISBN 0 00 599923 5

First published 1986

Data capture by Culham College Institute for Church Related Education
Phototypeset by Burgess & Son (Abingdon) Ltd
Printed in Great Britain by Bell and Bain Ltd., Glasgow

CONTENTS

Preface   *John M. Hull*   7

Foreword   *Leslie J. Francis*   10

Introduction   *Leslie J. Francis*   11

  1 Christian Nurture   *Leslie J. Francis*   13

  2 Children and Communion   *Leslie J. Francis*   22

  3 Family Services   *Leslie J. Francis*   32

  4 Small Villages   *Andrew Bowden*   41

  5 Large Churches   *John Duckett*   50

  6 Friday Club   *Paddy Phillips*   57

  7 Family Project Day   *Leslie J. Francis*   65

  8 Good Friday Project   *Doreen Storr*   72

  9 Teddy Bears   *Leslie J. Francis*   79

10 Church Primary Schools   *Leslie J. Francis*   88

11 Secular Secondary Schools   *Leslie J. Francis*   98

12 Dance   *Nicola Slee*   108

13 Music   *David Lankshear*   117

14 Speech and Drama   *Katherine Musson*   126

15 Poetry and Prose   *Nicola Slee*   137

16 Adult Groups   *Leslie J. Francis*   147

Notes on Contributors   156

Index   159

PREFACE

John M. Hull

It is ten years since the British Council of Churches published *The Child in the Church*. This report recommended that "the churches should give careful consideration to times, places and patterns of worship in order to effect the appropriate integration of children and adults" and "that gatherings of the local church for worship should be modified so that greater opportunity is created for the participation of children in ways appropriate to them and to the liturgy" (recommendations 10 and 11). Five years later, a sequel to *The Child in the Church* was published under the title *Understanding Christian Nurture*. The last chapter of this, 'Worship and Christian Nurture' made some progress in these directions, and it is now often remarked that those churches which continue to nurture their children separately from the activities of the main congregation are continuing to lose them, while churches where children are increasingly integrated into the congregational life are tending to keep them.

Phillip Cliff has provided us with a fascinating study of this problem in *The Rise and Development of the Sunday School Movement in England 1780–1980* (National Christian Education Council, 1986). It seems likely that the Sunday School Movement, which began as a general educational concern, and only became devoted to Christian nurture and evangelisation in the middle and later years of the nineteenth century, can be regarded as leading churches and Christian families away from a central truth. The main responsibility for the religious socialisation of children must be carried by the basic communities of faith and kinship to which these children belong. Christian children grow up in their families and their churches. Their growth and development cannot be made the responsibility of a more or less separate institution (the Sunday school). The whole of the local church is responsible for its children.

There is, in a sense, nothing particularly new about this insight. It can be found, expressed in various ways, throughout the history of the church. It is an emphasis, however, which has been growing since the end of the Second World War, especially in Protestant churches. In the United States, John H. Westerhoff is the leading contemporary exponent of this understanding of community-centred Christian nurture. His well-known book *Will our Children have Faith?*

was published in 1976, and a similar emphasis was already to be found in England in John Sutcliffe's *Learning Community* which had appeared in 1974.

This new book by Leslie Francis is thus part of a rich tradition and a growing emphasis. The author is well-known not only for his work on the attitudes of children in county schools towards religion, and as a psychologist specialising in the religious development of children and young people, but for his work in the area of Christian nurture. His teddy bears have become almost as well-known as he himself, as chapter 9 of this book reveals.

Leslie Francis gathers together his experiences in a number of parishes, and presents the work of several friends and colleagues who have worked in similar ways in Christian nurture and family worship over a period of years. The result is a very lively and readable book, bubbling with ideas, presented with enthusiasm and common sense, in a way which is both spiritually enriching and practically helpful. It is true that the book springs from an Anglican context, but congregations of all Christian traditions will find much of relevance here, and the book has an explicit ecumenical emphasis. It is also true that the experiences reported here spring mainly from rural or large country town situations rather than dealing with the problem of children in our larger industrial cities. Once again, however, the patterns suggested here will undoubtedly have a wider application. If there is an area of content which has been somewhat neglected, it might perhaps be found in world religions. The great variety of religious communities, representing the major world faiths, which are now to be found in the British Isles have yet to be drawn into the context of mutual religious nurture, and one suspects that an essential aspect of growing-up as a Christian in today's world must be the experience of learning from a great religious faith other than one's own.

In my recent book *What Prevents Christian Adults from Learning?* (SCM Press, 1985) I have tried to distinguish between that Christian education which proceeds from faith to faith within the Christian community (inner-ideological education), that which proceeds by way of dialogue between the Christian community and other religious traditions (inter-ideological education), and that which attempts some sort of critique of religion from the outside (extra-ideological education). This new book by Leslie Francis is a fine example of the first kind of approach. It speaks from faith to faith, and thus represents a valuable attempt to build up that faithful and secure identity without which the other forms of Christian nurture and education cannot get started.

Life in the churches in Britain today can be a rich and exciting experience for children and young people. This will not be the case, however, in churches where the needs of tired and embattled adults take absolute precedence over the needs of vital and growing children. Many adults have a genuine need for quiet meditation, peaceful silence, and for the tranquility of unchanging convention and undemanding repetition. The needs of such adults are not compatible with the needs of most children and young people, and we need now to give serious attention to how the needs of these adults can be met. What is becoming increasingly clear is that the normal weekly pattern of local church life cannot be expected to carry the weight of the needs of older and middle-aged adults.

If that continues to be the case, children and young people will continue to find such patterns of church life intolerably boring. We need a youthful church, a church where worship is characterised by participation, by variety, by lively music and by a socially involved spirituality. Let there be trumpets. Let there be joy. Let there be costly social commitment and a challenging identification with the poor and the oppressed. For those older adults who need to find in the church a place free of conflict and controversy, a place for introspection and individual, uninvolved worship, we need to create a new movement. We need to have occasional 'adult weekends' or infrequent 'adult services' instead of the sporadic 'family services' which, all too often, represent the grudging concession of an aging congregation to the needs of its younger families.

Perhaps the finest feature of Leslie Francis's book is its integration of life. The church, the school and the home, sacred and secular time, sacred and secular place, old and young (and middle-aged!), the various subjects of the curriculum, the senses, thinking and feeling, church and world, the seriousness and the frivolity of sacred play are all brought together in these pages to form one whole environment of Christian living. I am grateful for this opportunity to recommend this book and I believe that it will do much good in all the churches.

Faculty of Education   John M. Hull
University of Birmingham   Easter 1986

FOREWORD

I began to write this book as a natural history of the experiences through which my thinking about *Christian nurture* and *family worship* emerged in practice. Such a process has made me think carefully about the people who enabled me to have these experiences or to benefit from them. The foreword gives me the opportunity to say thank you to them: to Peter Walker and Margaret Wileman for giving me the freedom and confidence to pursue research; to Roger Stirrup for demonstrating the viability of a rural non-stipendiary ministry; to Bishop Leslie Brown for welcoming me into his diocese as a non-stipendiary deacon; to Canon Eric Graves for offering me a title; to the Venerable Kenneth Child for entrusting me with the non-stipendiary care of my own parishes; to the congregations of the five churches I have served for forgiving my mistakes and for growing with me; to Paul Jenkins for working with me on the issue of children and communion; to Nicola Slee for helping me to understand teddy bears and the place of anthology in the development of religious language; to Penny West for working with me on the relationship between liturgy and the local church school; to Doreen Storr for stimulating me to tell the tale of this book; to Andrew Bowden, John Duckett, David Lankshear, Katherine Musson, Paddy Phillips, Nicola Slee and Doreen Storr for contributing their own chapters; to John Gay and the Culham College Institute for encouraging me to develop the relationship between research and practice; to Kim Luckett for listening to my voice on tape and struggling with my script; to Christine Wright, Helen Hughes, Sally Knowles and Kathleen Mills for proof reading and commenting on my text; to Alan Davies for phototypesetting; but above all to my parents, whose own practice of Christian nurture seems to have borne some fruit.

Culham College Institute,   Leslie J. Francis
January 1986

INTRODUCTION

Leslie J. Francis

Both as a researcher and as a parish priest, I have become increasingly conscious of the growing gap between the church services I attend on Sunday and the majority of the people I meet going about their secular lives on Monday. The secularisation of the school system serves to widen this gap. The biggest challenge facing the churches in our society today is that of making contact with those who have grown up or who are growing up outside the churches.

To respond creatively to this challenge, I believe that our churches must begin by recognising and acknowledging just how wide the gap really is between our regular pattern of services and the young people growing up in a secular educational system. The next step is to identify the points of contact which already exist in most of our parishes, but which are not always used to good effect.

My aim in preparing this book is to draw attention to the various ways in which quite ordinary churches have worked to make contact with children and adults in the secular world. Half of the chapters tell the experiences of my own parishes; the other half are written by friends who share the same basic aims and enthusiasms. My own chapters began life when various groups invited me to tell the story behind some of my earlier books, like *His Spirit is With Us*. Then I recognised the way in which other people's stories complemented and corrected my own.

The twin themes running throughout this book are those of *family worship* and *Christian nurture*. Family worship attempts to extend the liturgy of the church to the children and adults on the fringes of church life. Christian nurture is the process through which the people of God attempt to enable another generation to become part of the life of the worshipping community. Christian nurture and family worship, therefore, go hand in hand as ways of making contact.

Chapter one makes plain some of the theory implicit behind the other chapters. It examines the reasons for placing the task of Christian nurture firmly in the hands of the church congregation, rather than in the day school or Sunday school. The following chapters each take one particular theme and examine it within a concrete context. My hope is that others will recognise something of their own situation in these contexts and be inspired and challenged to try out new ways of making contact for themselves.

While the chapters have been organised to provide a progressive sequence of thought, care has also been taken to make each chapter self-contained in its own right. This means that it is possible to use the book in a variety of ways. It is certainly not necessary to begin at the beginning and to read each chapter in turn, although some readers may prefer to do this.

The autonomy of the individual chapters should make the book particularly helpful for parish discussion groups and working groups. For example, if a local church is considering the issue of children and communion, or intending to organise a non-eucharistic family service, or planning a family project day, it should be possible to suggest to members of the Parochial Church Council, working party or planning group that they concentrate specifically on the appropriate chapter to provide some background for their discussion.

While this book begins with the specific experiences of its writers, its future now lies very much in the hands of the readers. Its potential will only be fulfilled if it succeeds in inspiring in new places experimentation and good practice in Christian nurture and family worship.

1 CHRISTIAN NURTURE

Leslie J. Francis

Context

The last decade has seen a considerable shift in Christian education towards the emphasis being placed on the rôle of the worshipping community or congregation. When I was a primary school child during the 1950s, the job of Christian education was clearly seen to be in the hands of the day schools and of the Sunday schools. Children did not seem particularly welcome in the church congregation and certainly the adult worshipping community was not prepared to make substantial concessions for the presence of the child in its midst. The move to the present emphasis on the rôle of the church congregation in Christian education goes hand in hand with fundamental changes in the day schools and the Sunday schools.

The subsequent chapters of this book describe imaginative ways in which church congregations have responded to welcoming children and unchurched adults into their services. This first chapter, however, concentrates on the principles behind such practice, by examining why churches can no longer leave the job of Christian education to day schools and Sunday schools.

Day schools

When the English educational system was refashioned after the Second World War the basic tenor of the 1944 Education Act was to design a Christian education system for a predominantly Christian country. In practice the churches were given three vital opportunities to influence the Christian character of the day school: daily collective worship was made a mandatory feature of school life in all state maintained schools; religious education was made the only component of the school curriculum compulsorily established by law; the churches were given the opportunity to continue their partnership in the state maintained system of schools through church voluntary aided and church voluntary controlled schools.

Against this background, as a child in the 1950s, I experienced no tension between church and school. My neighbourhood junior school happened to be a Church of England voluntary controlled school. All the children in my area began their school day with a Christian act of worship and our regular religious education lessons were bible-based. At school I learnt to say the prayers which were said in the local parish church, sing the hymns and some of the canticles which were sung in the local parish church and hear scripture read from the same translation as used in the local parish church. In the top year, the vicar came in once a week to teach the catechism.

Although the 1944 Education Act still governs the English educational system, the assumptions my parents made about Christian education taking place through the neighbourhood school no longer necessarily hold good. Over the last decade or two, educational theorists have been busy radically questioning all three religious provisions of the 1944 Education Act.

First, schools have become increasingly uncertain about the place of the daily act of worship. For example, John Hull's influential book, *School Worship: An obituary*, published in 1975, marshals a range of powerful arguments why schools should no longer expect their pupils to engage in acts of Christian worship. One thrust of this argument is that as England has become more culturally and religiously plural, so it is inappropriate for schools to promote any one specific form of religious worship. A second thrust of this argument is that as England has become more and more secular, so schools cannot assume any religious background in their pupils and thus it is inappropriate for the secular school to foster participation in a religious tradition among pupils who are not accustomed to such practice at home. A third thrust of this argument is that worship presupposes commitment to a belief system, while schools should be in the business of stimulating not belief but critical questioning.

Second, while religious education remains a fixed part of the school timetable, what takes place in religious education lessons has radically changed direction. What is now carried out as religious education by many professionals in the field would not have been recognised as such by the churches who pressed for the compulsory provision of religious education at the time of the 1944 Education Act. Today the aim of religious education is seen not in *confessional* terms of making pupils religious, but in *educational* terms of making pupils critically informed about religion.

Third, the whole question of the distinctiveness of church schools has been subjected to close scrutiny not only by national secularist bodies, but also by educational philosophers. A clear exponent of such a position is Professor Paul Hirst, who holds the chair of education at the University of Cambridge. For example in his paper 'Education, Catechesis and the Church School', Hirst argues that catechesis and education just do not mix, and should not be seen to be taking place in the same context.

Of course, there remains a significant time lapse between developments in educational theory and changes in school practice. Christian education is still far from dead in the state maintained system of schools; but it would now be very unwise for the churches to assume that state maintained schools will continue to share their task of Christian nurture.

Sunday schools

Historically the Sunday school movement grew up alongside the day school movement. Many Sunday schools began in the eighteenth and nineteenth centuries to provide a basic grounding in reading, writing and arithmetic, as well as in religion. Before the 1870 Education Act Sunday schools may well have been the only educational opportunities available to young people in some areas. Clearly, this aspect of Sunday schools has outlived its usefulness. The idea that Sunday schools exist as a parallel provision for young people alongside church services for adult worshippers has also run into practical and theoretical difficulties since my own childhood.

In practical terms, many churches have found it difficult to maintain their Sunday schools, and this for a range of reasons. First, secularisation itself has taken its toll. As fewer parents attend church, so fewer parents are concerned to send their children to Sunday school. Cars, televisions and changes in leisure patterns have all helped to accentuate the secularisation process away from the churches on Sunday.

Second, the expectations of young people themselves have changed, even among those from churchgoing families. The vast changes that have taken place in the day schools, in terms of school buildings, curriculum materials and professional practices, have all tended to raise the child's expectations of education. Often the Sunday school is unable to compete with the child's expectations of secular education. Church vestries sometimes compare unfavourably with purpose-built classrooms; economically produced catechetical materials sometimes compare unfavourably with sophisticated secular learning materials; untrained or semi-trained volunteer teachers sometimes compare unfavourably with the trained and skilled professionals of the day school.

Third, the secularisation of the day school has tended to make the Sunday school teachers' task more difficult. The Sunday school teacher can no longer assume a child's basic familiarity, from the experience of the day school, with formerly well-known bible stories, with the hymns regularly sung in the local church and with traditional Christian prayers.

In theoretical terms, the churches have begun to re-examine what it is precisely that their Sunday schools can achieve. For many churches the experience of running autonomous Sunday schools is that they tend to act as an end in themselves. Instead of preparing young people for adult church membership, Sunday schools have tended to lose their pupils around the ages of nine or ten and these pupils have not begun to fill the gap by going to church services instead of attending Sunday school.

Congregations

The British Council of Churches report, *The Child in the Church*, published in 1976, challenged the churches to rethink their work among children and young people. The central theses of this report are that Christian nurture is the responsibility of the local congregation and that Christian nurture involves the active integration of the child within the worshipping community. These twin theses have two profound implications.

The first implication of these recommendations is that each active and committed member of the congregation is invited to recognise his or her personal responsibility to the local church's programme of Christian nurture. The Christian nurture of the young can no longer be delegated to the specialist or left in the hands of one or two particular volunteers. The corollary is that the blame for the local church's failure in Christian nurture can no longer be passed down the line to the vicar or to the Sunday school teachers. The mature and responsible congregation needs to accept the brief for the Christian nurture programme of the church as part of the individual members' own baptismal commitment.

The way in which individuals can respond to this invitation will vary greatly. There is one sense in which all members of the congregation are already completely equipped for their rôle in the Christian nurture of the young by virtue of their very membership of the worshipping community. In this sense, Christian nurture is literally about sharing the life of the worshipping community with others, and first and foremost this means individual members being open and willing to share themselves. An alert congregation needs to spot the resources which it already possesses in its members and to deploy these resources wisely.

In another sense, however, the organisation of the local church's Christian nurture programme can be a very costly process. Each local worshipping community needs specialist skills if it is to build a secure basis for the nurture of its young members. The children who receive professional education in their secular day schools have the right to receive just as professional treatment in their programme of Christian nurture. Congregations, therefore, need individuals who are willing to be trained as resource persons. The task of these resource persons is not to *do* the Christian nurture on behalf of the congregation, but to become the effective enablers, who can release the potential of the full worshipping community and so enable the church to fulfil its function more adequately in Christian nurture.

At the same time, each local worshipping community needs the appropriate buildings and educational resources to work effectively among children and young people; and these cost money. The church which does not allocate an appropriate budget for its

Christian nurture programme has already signalled the lack of seriousness it attributes to this area of its life.

The second implication of these recommendations is that churches should plan and organise their regular pattern of worship to integrate fully both children and adults. Children are not mini-adults and cannot be expected to participate meaningfully in a form of activity organised with only the needs of adults in mind. Nor is the child to be seen solely as the church of tomorrow. The child is just as much part of the church of today as the adult members and, on this basis, should be just as much taken into account in influencing the character of the worshipping community.

The way in which individual churches can respond to this call to think seriously about the place of the child in the congregation can vary greatly. At one level, the process needs to begin simply by making children and young people feel welcome. The worshipping community which extends to children and young people a feeling of welcoming warmth, love, security and acceptance has already taken a firm initiative along the path of Christian nurture.

At another level, however, the local church needs to go much further than this and actively to encourage changes in the very shape of its services in order to recognise the unique contribution of its younger members. The worship of the local church needs to be structured so that opportunities are given for the participation of children and young people in ways appropriate both to them and to the liturgy. Much of the rest of this book explores concrete examples of how the family worship of the church can actively take into account the demands of Christian nurture.

Christian nurture

The notion of *nurture* is something quite different from the notion of *education*. The notion of Christian nurture is something quite different from both Christian education and religious education. The concept of education, as defined for example by educational philosophers like Professor Paul Hirst, is concerned with the development of the mind and with the aim of rational autonomy. Nurture is a much wider concept. Nurture enables the child to grow and to develop, while Christian nurture enables the child to grow and to develop within the Christian tradition. This implies nurture in patterns of behaviour, attitudes, values and beliefs, as well as in intellectual understanding. Christian nurture is more than education about the Christian faith: it is an introduction to the culture and to the way of life that makes Christian people different from those who are not Christian. At the heart of this difference is the idea of the people of God as a worshipping people, celebrating their awareness of living in God's world through the liturgy of the church.

Having drawn a distinction between nurture and education, it is equally important to draw a distinction between nurture and indoctrination. To indoctrinate is to pass on values, beliefs and practices in an uncritical way. Christian nurture strenuously resists this temptation. Five years after the report *The Child in the Church*, the British Council of Churches produced a sequel, *Understanding Christian Nurture*, which examines in some detail the need to draw a sharp distinction between nurture and indoctrination. This second report argues that indoctrination is a closed process, while nurture is 'critically open', and that critical openness is at the very heart of the Christian tradition in the questing and testing of faith. Christian nurture would, in effect, be untrue to the Christian tradition if it did not involve the fundamental values of critical openness.

The translation of this abstract concept of Christian nurture into concrete programmes which can be handled by church congregations involves thinking through three different issues, which embrace theological, psychological and educational principles.

The theological argument is that the primary purpose of Christian nurture is not merely that the child should possess a body of knowledge about the bible, about the history of the faith, or about the content of doctrine. Nor is it merely that the child should be familiar with and encouraged to adopt the Christian ethic or code of behaviour. These are most certainly not the starting points. Both knowledge and behaviour are secondary to a sense of belonging to the Christian community and of feeling part of that community when it is celebrating its distinctive identity.

First and foremost, therefore, I wish to nurture the child into feeling part of the community that celebrates the eucharist, for it is here that encounter with the living Christ illuminates and authenticates the voice of scripture, the traditions of the church and the Christian code of conduct. Subsequently, the child will want to ask about and to discover the implications of being part of that community in terms of beliefs and behaviour.

The psychological argument is that we need to take seriously the developmental stages in the growth cycle of young people. This should help to shape our expectations for different age groups and the kind of learning situations we prepare for them. Against this background, it is helpful to distinguish clearly the nurturing needs of three different age groups, and to be aware of the intermediate age ranges between these groups.

The first group is the pre-schooler, the child up to the age of five. The primary focus for Christian nurture among this age group is to enable the child to feel at home in church, to feel loved by the worshipping community and to feel secure among them. The pre-schooler needs the welcome of a crèche, rather than the structured programme of the classroom.

The second group is the junior child between the ages of seven and eleven. The primary focus of Christian nurture among this age group is on attitude formation. At this stage attitudes are beginning to determine the areas in which the child will concentrate attention and about which he or she will learn to think maturely at a later stage. Unless positive attitudes are being developed towards the church at this age, little real learning is likely to take place for some years subsequently. The junior child needs to like the worship of the church rather than, as yet, to understand it.

The third group is the upper secondary child, from the age of fourteen or fifteen onwards. The primary focus of Christian nurture among this age group is on relationships and values. At this stage personal identity is being established through social interaction and the practical implications of competing value structures are being explored. Unless the church is seen to validate its gospel by implementing its ideals in social practice and by giving time to take the individual seriously, little real interest will be shown in the teaching and theory underpinning the church's identity. The teenager needs to experience the gospel in practice, in personal and social terms, before he or she will take an interest in theology.

The educational argument is that the teaching methods and materials employed in the cause of Christian nurture must be consistent with the expectations the child forms from his or her experience of the best secular education. The child needs to discover that what he or she most enjoys about secular education has a rightful and respected place within the Christian community. In other words, the church needs to be aware of the fact that it is the secular school which teaches the child how to learn.

In practice, this means that the pre-schooler's crèche must compete with the range of facilities and activities offered by the local playschools. The junior child's nurture programme must draw upon the wide range of discovery learning and organised projects so familiar in the primary school classroom. The teenager's nurture programme must learn from the experience learning techniques employed in the secondary school, including the exploration of social issues and personal growth through drama, role play, poetry, prose and open discussion. On this account, Christian nurture is not about a different kind of educational activity, but about bringing the familiar aspects of education into contact with the worshipping community and with the Christ who stands at the centre of the worship.

So much, then, for theory. Each of the following chapters tells a story to show aspects of this theory in practice.

2 CHILDREN AND COMMUNION

Leslie J. Francis

Context

I began my ministry serving as a non-stipendiary deacon in a rapidly expanding 'overspill' town of some 15,000 inhabitants. The medieval parish church stood at the centre of what had been, until quite recently, a small Suffolk market town. Now new estates were springing up in all directions and the indigenous Suffolk population was being swamped by new-comers, mainly from London.

At the same time, I was working on a doctoral research project in Cambridge, studying the religious development of school children. Not surprisingly, therefore, I took a particular interest in the way in which my parish church was relating to children and young people. It seemed to me that the parish church was sending out two very clear, but contradictory, messages to children of primary school age and to their parents.

The message sent out by the pastoral theory of the parish was that the life of the church centred on the Sunday morning Parish Communion. The Parish Communion was the characteristic activity which brought together the people of God in the parish and gave them their unique identity. Children, it was said, were an important part of the people of God and, therefore, had an integral place in the Parish Communion. In principle the parish agreed with the notion that children are not just part of the church of tomorrow, but an essential ingredient of the church of today.

The message sent out by the pastoral practice of the parish was that the Sunday morning service was an adult activity, staged by adults for adults. Children who came to the Parish Communion were left very much on the fringe of the service. Because they did not feel part of what was going on, they became bored and behaved restlessly. Their parents were made to feel uncomfortable, embarrassed and angry. The overall result was that both the children and their parents stayed away from church on Sunday.

The church has an incredible problem on its hands when it tries to cater for all ages and for all tastes in one major Sunday service. It must be the only organisation left that tries to cater for two year olds and eighty year olds, for senior graduate executives and for unemployed school leavers, for long standing members and for raw recruits, all at the same time and all in the same way. There is something in our theology which alerts us to the ideal of such an aim. But there is also something in our experience which must tell us how seriously the aim fails in practice.

Desirable as it may be from the point of view of young children and their parents, it is plainly not feasible to make all liturgy child-centred. The senior members of the congregation also have the right to expect their needs to be recognised and addressed within the liturgy. The appropriate form of compromise seemed to be to set aside special Sundays, say the first Sunday in the month, to take seriously the needs of young children and their parents, while catering for other sections of the congregation just as explicitly on other Sundays.

Children of different ages understandably have different needs. I came to see children of primary school age, five to eleven year olds, to be particularly important from the point of view of influencing the shape of the Parish Communion. Children who have not yet begun to go to school are probably going to find church services rather strange anyway. What pre-schoolers really need is to be cared for and loved within an adjacent crèche, or given the fairly constant attention of their parents throughout the service. Children who have grown into the pattern of secondary education are more able to take a full part in an adult service. But what of the five to eleven year olds?

Five to eleven year olds

As I watched the five to eleven year olds in the congregation of my church, three main principles began to clarify in my mind.

First, children of this age need to be present at the Parish Communion as active participants, not as mere spectators or observers of something done for them by adults. This does not mean that children have to be admitted to receive the sacrament at this age. It does mean that they should be encouraged to participate throughout the liturgy.

In some ways the important theological question of admitting children to receive the sacrament can become a dangerous distraction from the practical question of understanding how children can fully participate throughout the whole service. I have been present at services where young children have received communion and yet felt themselves to be sitting on the outside of an all-adult activity. I have been present at other services where children of this age have experienced no problem in not receiving the sacrament, because they have been totally aware of the key part they themselves have played in preparing for and conducting the whole service. In many cases these children find themselves kneeling at the altar rail alongside adults who have not yet been admitted to communion either.

Second, children of this age cannot be treated as miniature and incomplete adults. This age group has an integrity and wholeness all of its own, quite different from the integrity and wholeness of adults, but no less valuable in its own right. This means that we need to start with the question "what are children of this age like?" not with the question "which adult tasks in the church can be delegated to children?" It is true that children like to ring the bell, carry the processional cross, sing in the choir and take part in the offertory procession, but this should not provide our starting point.

The better starting point is to observe carefully the practice of the primary schools these children attend during the week. It is from their experience of the primary school that children actually learn how to learn. For example, their introduction to music may well be through playing percussion instruments and dancing, rather than through listening to the organ and standing in straight rows. Their idea of singing praises to God may well be influenced by the example of the BBC Radio for Schools hymn book, *Come and Praise*, rather than the plainsong of *The English Hymnal* or the four part harmony of *Hymns Ancient and Modern*. Their ability to grasp new information may well come through making a model rather than from listening to a lecture.

Third, children of this age cannot be expected to handle books designed primarily for adults. During the past few decades educational research has made great strides in understanding children's reading capabilities, their concentration span and even their ability to hold and to handle books. As a result of this research a quiet revolution has taken place in the design of the best educational books. This means that liturgy arranged primarily with five to eleven year olds in mind needs to develop its own liturgical books. These books should be useful, easy to use, fun to handle and good to look at.

To be useful children's liturgical books need to contain all the material which is going to be used in the service. To be easy to use the books need to be typeset in a clear typeface and carefully designed, taking note of line length, speech rhythms, the appropriate stages to turn the pages and the use of open space. It is also important that the child is not distracted or confused by rubrics, explanations or alternative texts.

To be fun to handle the books have to be in the correct proportion both for child-sized hands and for church-sized pew ledges. Too large a book may spend much of its time on the floor with the child often burrowing under the pews to retrieve it! To be good to look at the books need high quality, full colour illustrations. For the young reader the illustrations will complement the significance of the text. For the pre-reader and for the slow reader the illustrations will give immediate access to the ideas underlying what is as yet inaccessible text.

Illustrations

As a consequence of these observations, I began to plan a children's communion book, with the help of a friend, the Reverend Paul Jenkins. Paul brought to the project both his professional training as a primary school teacher and his skill as an artist. Together we came to see that the Parish Communion we celebrated in our churches could be analysed into thirty-one sections or key components and that each of these components could be enriched by a carefully chosen picture.

A good starting point to give as an example of what we had in mind is the prayer of intercessions and thanksgivings. This prayer divides up very easily into six sections: the invitation to prayer, the prayer for the church, the prayer for the nations of the world, the prayer for the local neighbourhood, the prayer for the sick and for those who suffer and the prayer remembering those who have died in the faith of Christ.

Each of these six sections of the prayer of intercessions and thanksgivings suggests a very clear double page illustration. The prayer for the church suggests the people of God assembled as the worshipping community, with their priest and bishop. The prayer for the nations of the world suggests an international, multiracial, multicultural mix of people, characterised by their cultural differences in dress and food. The prayer for the local neighbourhood suggests the people who make our neighbourhood what it is: the postman, the milkman, the young and the old. The prayer for the sick and for those who suffer suggests the child's cut knee and the hospital bed; it suggests the skilled care of doctors and nurses.

The prayer remembering those who have died in the faith of Christ is more problematic. To begin with, Paul and I considered designing a picture of saints and of people of past ages. We rejected this idea because it seemed to be putting the emphasis in the wrong place. We did not want to communicate the ideas either that the Kingdom of God is reserved for special heroes, like the saints remembered by name within the church, or that those who have died in the faith of Christ remain locked into a past age, as an anachronism from today's perspective. Instead, we wanted to communicate the idea that we are actually sharing life in Christ with the whole of his church, living and departed.

Working alongside children, we discovered that three images in particular helped us to make the point regarding the continuity of the life which is within Christ. The first image is that of light, which the child discovers exists in a variety of forms. The second image is that of the butterfly which symbolises both the transformation of life and the essential continuity of life between the egg, the caterpillar, the chrysalis and the butterfly itself. The third image is the one St Paul uses of the seed being planted and leading to new springtime growth. Consequently, we have experimented with three different illustrations for this section: a delightful picture of candles, of butterflies in flight and of children tending a garden in Spring.

Finally, we decided to illustrate the invitation to prayer with a picture of children enjoying a range of activities. The message we wanted to convey here was that prayer is not so much a catalogue of requests, as a conversation between friends. In this conversation God cares about what is important to us. Believe it or not, God actually wants to listen to our story about the happenings of the day.

Another easy example of the natural divisions within the communion service is the way in which the Nicene Creed logically divides into three sections, as we confess our faith in God the creator, Christ the saviour and the Holy Spirit the giver of life. Belief in God the Father is symbolised by the flame of the burning bush through which he made himself known in the Old Testament to Moses. Belief in God the Son is symbolised by the cross. Belief in God the Holy Spirit is symbolised by the wind through which he made himself known at Pentecost.

Projects

Giving children their own specially designed communion book is only the start. They then need to discover how this book can help them to participate fully in the celebration of the liturgy.

The next stage in my quest to help children feel at home in the Parish Communion was to develop a series of project-based learning experiences. I wanted to use project learning because this is something with which children are familiar through their secular schooling. The key is to relate this kind of learning programme to the regular celebration of the eucharist. The thirty-one pictures which Paul and I developed for the children's communion book provided the ideal link. We wanted to enable the children to make clear associations between the project learning and these pictures. Through the pictures the experience of the projects began to enrich and to inform the children's participation in the eucharist.

We envisaged that children of the primary school age range could work on the projects in a number of different contexts. If the child-centred Parish Communion is happening on the first Sunday in the month, the children could work on their project throughout the remaining Sundays in the church hall, while a more traditional service is being conducted in the church. Alternatively 'project workshops' can take place in parents' homes, the vestry, the church hall, after hours in the local school or in the church itself. Project workshops can be arranged to last just half an hour on Sunday, an hour or so after school in the week, for a whole day at weekends, or during the school holidays. A number of small groups can meet throughout the week at different times and in different places, as proves most convenient to the children and the organisers. The groups are given a unity by working on a common theme. Where a church aided primary school is associated with the parish, it is possible to organise projects in the school itself.

Whenever and wherever the projects take place, the important thing is to link the learning of the project with the celebration of the church's liturgy by seeing that the project reaches its climax in the Parish Communion itself. The church building becomes the place in which the project is displayed, and the intention of the eucharist becomes the offering of this project to God. The celebration of the liturgy is where the secular and the sacred meet.

By way of an example of how all this works in practice, I return to the third section of the creed, where we state our belief in God the Holy Spirit. The illustration Paul and I designed for the children's communion book shows a group of children flying kites on a windy day. This illustration has been chosen because wind is one of the primary Christian images for God the Holy Spirit. The link is made most obvious in the languages of the bible, both Hebrew and Greek, where the same word stands both for wind and for spirit.

In the project associated with this part of the service, we have explored the many facets of the wind. We have made kites and taken them out to fly them. We have made a video film of our kites flying in the park and getting caught up in the branches of the trees. We have made windmills of all shapes and sizes and taken a coach trip to see a working windmill in action.

We have looked at photographs of the windmills in Holland

and made a collage illustrating them. We have blown up balloons and had a party with them. We have filled balloons with gas and sent them off floating over the countryside bearing a message. We have visited the reservoir to see sailing boats manoeuvre and made large models of sails and rigging. We have made balsa wood gliders and talked with the churchwarden who pilots his own glider. We have looked at aeroplanes and talked with a wartime pilot. We have made a model hot air balloon and lived the excitement of travelling round the world by balloon in 80 days.

We have pretended that we were out on the mountains struggling against the gale, or on some tropical island basking in the warm breeze. We have danced the dance of leaves caught up in the wind. We have written stories and poems about the wind and painted pictures. We have studied how the wind blows washing inside out and shakes apples from the trees. We have seen how wind rustles through the branches, how breath brings the recorder to life and how the church organ depends on bellows. By doing these things we have learnt about the mysterious movement of the Holy Spirit. And along the way we have encountered extracts from scripture, as well as modern and traditional hymns about God the Holy Spirit. We have produced an anthology of useful material.

Finally, we have taken the results of our project to church on Sunday and we have summed them all up at the Parish Communion. Here we have celebrated our work and shared our experiences with the whole worshipping community as that community comes together to celebrate its faith in the Christ of the eucharist. Through that eucharist we have offered our work to God in worship. A hot air balloon has been hung from the pulpit; flags waved from the rood screen; kites fluttered from the rafters. A windmill has stood on the font. Balloons have been suspended above the pews and let down at the end of the service. Our drawings, poems and stories have been mounted; the photographs of our visit to the park, the windmill and the reservoir have been displayed. A wind-band has come to accompany the hymns. Adult dancers have presented their dance of the wind at the offertory. Choral speech, drama and song have been integrated into the service. The members of the congregation have been presented with a booklet of reflections on God the Holy Spirit to take home after the service.

Through this kind of project all sorts of people have been caught up in the job of Christian nurture. The churchwarden who never dreamed of teaching in Sunday school enjoyed sharing with children his experience as a glider pilot. The mother who knew nothing about theology knew how to teach the making of kites. The neighbourhood wind-band which had no contact with the church was delighted to play at the 'wind' celebration when the project reached its climax in church. The family who had spent a holiday in Holland enjoyed sharing slides of the windmills they had seen. The schoolteacher who had no confidence in teaching scripture had no hesitation in running a classroom project on sailing boats through the ages.

Children have enjoyed their project on the Spirit. Their families and friends have enjoyed seeing their work contribute to the celebration of the Parish Communion. Most of all, each time the third section of the creed is recited, the illustration of flying kites will remind them of the mysterious wind-like quality of God the Holy Spirit.

Conclusion

By developing projects of this nature for all thirty-one sections of the communion service, I found it possible over a period of time both to develop the child's understanding of the worship of the church and to encourage five to eleven year olds actually to look forward to coming to the Parish Communion. Gradually the barriers between the secular and the sacred are dissolved, and the child feels at home in church.

Note

The picture communion book arranged by Paul Jenkins and Leslie J. Francis is available in several editions: *The Lord is Here!* uses the Order for Holy Communion Rite A from *The Alternative Service Book 1980*; *The Lord be with you!* uses the Order of Holy Communion Rite B from *The Alternative Service Book 1980*; *At the Lord's Table* (Ireland) uses An Order for the Celebration of The Holy Communion from *The Alternative Prayer Book 1984*; *At the Lord's Table* (Australia) *uses the Second Order for the Holy Communion from An Australian Prayer Book. His Spirit is with us: a project approach to Christian nurture* by Leslie J. Francis provides a programme of teaching material to develop children's understanding of the pictures in these communion books and to enrich their experience of the communion service.

3 FAMILY SERVICES

Leslie J. Francis

Context

In one sense I have always wanted the main focus of the Sunday worship of my churches to be the Parish Communion. The flexibility of the eucharistic rites in *The Alternative Service Book 1980* allows a great variety in the ways in which the Parish Communion can be presented. On some occasions the Parish Communion can be free and child-centred. An abbreviated rite can give space for young people to prepare an extended ministry of the word in song, dance and drama. Opportunities can be given for young people to create their own prayers of intercessions and thanksgivings and to prepare a nave table for the eucharistic prayer. On other occasions the Parish Communion can be completely formal and traditional in its presentation.

The great strength is that these two extremes are bound together with the same basic structure and the same essential components. The continuity between the child-centred presentation and the traditional presentation of the Parish Communion is expressed through actually using, for example, the same collect for purity and the same eucharistic prayer. Essentially the worshipping community is participating in the same characteristic liturgy of the people of God, presented in two rather different ways.

At the same time, I have also needed to recognise that the Parish Communion is not the appropriate form of liturgy to meet all the worship needs of the local church. There is a range of situations in which a different liturgical form is necessary and in which it is equally inappropriate to use the only authorised alternatives presented in *The Alternative Service Book 1980*, the offices of Morning Prayer and Evening Prayer in all their various forms. It is this experienced need for a form of liturgy not included in either *The Book of Common Prayer* or *The Alternative*

Service Book 1980 which stimulates Anglican parishes to experiment with forms of 'Family Services'.

Discovery

After I had been in one of my rural parishes for some time, the Parochial Church Council decided to review the pattern of services so we could try to assess whether the village church was ministering to the local community in the most useful way. Being a small village in a multiple parish benefice, the church could muster the resources for only one service each Sunday. On the first Sunday in the month the service was an early Holy Communion, on the second and fourth Sundays there was a mid-morning Parish Communion and on the third Sunday there was a late morning Matins. It was Matins which attracted the smallest congregation, so we began to speculate about replacing it with a Family Service. A small group was set up to discuss the question, consult village opinion and explore possibilities. A range of important considerations began to emerge.

First, we considered that there were a number of adults and children living in the community who were on the fringes of the village church. These were people who showed goodwill towards the church by coming to the carol service and to the harvest supper and who supported a stall at the Summer fête, but who neither looked nor felt totally at home in the Parish Communion or Matins on the rare occasions when they came.

We came to appreciate the fact that there exists a considerable cultural barrier between the formal liturgy of the church and the families growing up in a secular society. People who have not been nurtured into the life of the Church of England sit uneasily with so much of the imagery and language which constitutes traditional liturgy. For these fringe members to be integrated into the life of the local church there is an urgent need for some gentle bridge which enables the transition to be made from the secular to the religious culture in a way which is almost unnoticed. Family Services need to be able to act as this bridge.

Second, we quickly realised that the Church of England did not have a religious monopoly within the community. Although there were no other chapels or church buildings in the village, some of the people inhabiting the fringes of church life claimed nominal allegiance, if at all, to other Christian traditions. Their memories and expectations of church services may be quite different from those of nominal Anglicans. At the same time, we recognised that there was living within the heart of the community a skilled Methodist local preacher who needed to travel some distance for his own particular brand of Sunday worship. We invited him to join our working party and to contribute to a monthly 'United Family Service'. Joining resources with the resident Methodist local preacher increased the pastoral effectiveness of the enterprise greatly, especially given the fact that both the Anglican priest and reader lived in neighbouring villages.

Third, we needed to listen to the voice of the older or more established Anglicans within the community, those in fact who were about to lose their monthly Matins. The talk of an ecumenical venture gave rise to fears in some that the parish church would be completely departing from a recognised liturgical structure on the third Sunday in the month. My own view was that a united service should neither adopt the theoretically unstructured pattern of the Free Church tradition, nor follow directly the liturgical pattern from the Anglican Prayer Book. We needed to find a compromise position in which the strengths of both Anglicanism and the Free Churches could meet. In practice this meant seeking a specific liturgical structure, but a liturgical structure which would permit a great deal of flexibility.

Fourth, we decided that a monthly Family Service should try to reflect the life and the potential of the community itself as well as the views of the vicar and of the Methodist local preacher. We wanted to anchor the Family Service in a house group which existed to take responsibility for the planning. The group was to be as open as possible, specifically inviting some people to certain meetings and hoping and praying that others would come as well.

The task of of this planning group was to decide the theme and to plan the content of the monthly service. This meant preparing music, drama and proclamation, as well as choosing hymns and readings. The planning group was free to involve individuals and societies from the village, like the playgroup or the Women's

Institute, as appropriate ideas and occasions arose. Again we realised that planning a full fifty minute unstructured service from scratch is incredibly time-consuming and wasteful of resources. Yet another argument seemed to indicate the desirability of finding a regular liturgical pattern which would allow the planning group to assume certain consistencies from month to month, but at the same time give them the opportunity for creative development.

The precedents which we found in neighbouring churches for a liturgical structure to a Family Service were of two main kinds. Some followed a pattern derived from Matins, making use of an opening bidding, versicles, responses and perhaps the Venite. Others relied heavily on the creation of new material. Neither route seemed entirely satisfactory for our own situation. The problem with both models is that they fail to lead into the mainstream life of the worshipping community.

The danger in creating a form of Family Service which is so dissimilar from what the local church is doing in its other services is that the Family Service tends to build up a congregation of its own which remains isolated from the rest of the local church. The Family Service congregation still feels out of place at other church services, even if they are held in the same building! In other words, if one of the major aims of the Family Service is to build a bridge between the unchurched and the life of the local church, we must make sure that this bridge actually leads somewhere and does not merely become an end in itself.

Structure

These considerations led us to design a Family Service made up entirely from the components of the Rite A eucharist which the church would be using on the other Sundays in the month. The service which we designed included four main sections. The first section, Preparation, followed a formal pattern. The second, Ministry of the Word, allowed complete freedom. The third section, Prayers, combined the opportunity for creative freedom with a liturgical structure. The fourth section, Conclusion, like the opening section, followed a formal pattern.

In designing this form of service we deliberately did not write into the structure fixed places for hymns. We envisaged that often we would want an opening hymn before the Preparation, two or three hymns somewhere in the Ministry of the Word and a closing hymn between the Prayers and the Conclusion. We felt it important, however, to allow the specific theme chosen for individual services to determine the points within the liturgical framework where hymns would be most appropriate.

Generally our Family Services open with an informal word of welcome, the announcement of the theme for the day and an opening hymn. Then the first section of the service, the Preparation, follows this fixed pattern:

Greeting   We begin the Family Service with the greeting 'The Lord be with you', in exactly the same way as we begin the Parish Communion.

Opening prayer (collect for purity)   The opening prayer also follows the pattern of the Parish Communion as a preparation for worship.

Collect   The collect for the day, or a special prayer chosen to reflect the theme of the service, follows on immediately from the collect for purity. The collect is placed in this early position, well in advance of the Ministry of the Word, to demonstrate how the theme of the day has a vital part in the formal liturgical structure of the opening.

Prayers of penitence   The kyrie and confession examine our relationship with God early on in the service. The words of absolution celebrate the forgiveness which enables us to approach God and worship him in confidence.

Peace   The peace follows on immediately from the confession and absolution, demonstrating that the restoration of right relationship with God is also reflected in right relationships one with another. The peace gives the congregation the opportunity to greet one another and to relax in greater informality.

The second part of the service, the Ministry of the Word, is totally unstructured and left to the ministers or planning group to design differently for each occasion. As a rule, the Ministry of the Word includes hymns, one or two passages from scripture and a variety of other material, but the order in which these come depends on the total structure of what the planning group intends to include in the service.

The third section of the Family Service, the Prayers, again follows a formal pattern from the Rite A eucharist. This section is made up of two parts:

Prayer of intercessions and thanksgivings   The prayer of intercession and thanksgiving allows us to follow a fixed pattern of praying for the church, for the world, for our community, for the sick and suffering and for the departed. At the same time this pattern of prayer allows plenty of freedom for the development of specific intentions suggested by the overall theme of each family service.

Lord's prayer   We conclude the prayers by joining together in the Christian family prayer.

The prayers tend to lead into the final hymn, usually chosen to tie in with the theme of the day. Then the final part of the Family Service, the Conclusion, contains two components:

Praise   We want to end the Family Service on a note of praise and choose for this purpose the ancient canticle 'Glory to God in the highest'. This is the climax towards which the direction of the Family Service moves.

Blessing and dismissal   The service ends, as it begins, in exactly the same way as the Parish Communion, with the blessing and dismissal.

In selecting these particular components from the Rite A eucharist to form the structure of our liturgical Family Service, we were careful not to assume too much of the congregation. We invite the congregation to share in the confession, the peace, the prayer of intercessions and thanksgivings and the Lord's prayer. We do not, however, include the creed in our regular form of Family Service on the grounds that not everyone present can be assumed to want to identify with such a sharp statement of faith. On occasions when the theme of the service gives special point to a profession of faith, the creed can always be included in the context of the Ministry of the Word and follow on naturally from specific teaching. We were also careful to choose the words of the peace not to assume that the congregation only included those who could say 'we were all baptised into one body'. Part of our hope was that the unbaptised would be present at this form of service as well!

Having agreed this form of service, we recognised that we needed to produce appropriate material for use in the pews. On the one hand we realised that the hymns and other material specific to the theme of the day would need to be printed out specially for each service. On the other hand, we wanted the continuity of the liturgical framework from month to month to be very apparent. Our solution was to produce an order of service booklet which would contain all the basic material used each time and in the clearest and most accessible manner possible. We wanted to make the service booklet attractive for young children as well as for their parents, and so designed it to include a set of simple illustrations.

Our final consideration was to find a name for this form of service which we had created. Our working title had been 'Family Worship'; but the more we thought about the title, the more uneasy we became. The emphasis on Family Services in today's church seems to ignore the large part of the worshipping community and of the potential worshipping community who are not members of a conventional family structure. As a bachelor priest I became especially aware of the number of adults in the worshipping community living single lives. I also recognised the number of children from one parent families. After considerable reflection we decided to call our order of service simply *Come and Worship!*

Practice

The service booklet *Come and Worship!* was used as the regular structure for the monthly Family Service. Experience of using this form of service suggests that it adequately meets the needs we had identified. On the one hand, those familiar with the liturgical structure of Anglican worship found the framework sufficient to anchor their participation in the monthly Family Service. On the other hand, the Methodist local preacher, coming from an entirely different tradition, did not feel himself hidebound by the structure. The planning group found that they had lots of decisions to make and material to prepare for the Ministry of the Word, without being overwhelmed by having to structure from scratch a full fifty minute service each month. Children and adults on the fringes of church life felt able to participate easily in the monthly Family Service, without being expected either to know much about the regular liturgical structure of Anglican worship or to assent to too many implicit or explicit religious assumptions. Moreover, they also discovered that when they came to a Parish Communion service, on one of the other Sundays in the month or at the major Christian festivals, they were already familiar with much of the service.

During a typical month the *Come and Worship!* service would actively involve quite a large number of people from the community, not only in preparation beforehand but also in leading the service itself. A lay person who had taken a particular responsibility in structuring the theme for the day might well come forward from his or her seat to welcome the congregation, announce the theme and lead into the opening hymn. Another lay person might lead the formal opening of the service.

Next, the Ministry of the Word could involve a range of skills from the local community. The theme of the day might include a short piece of drama worked out by three or four adults. Children might have been invited beforehand to prepare a song or to offer a picture or a model. The planning group might have decided to include a passage from scripture or from a novel to be read by a range of voices spread out around the church building. Sometimes pre-recorded music might be played or a sequence of pictures or slides used. Sometimes the prayer of intercessions and thanksgivings might be divided up among five voices, each preparing a short bidding for the distinct sections of the prayer. On some occasions the Methodist local preacher or I would decide that we wanted to include a more traditional teaching ministry, involving a short sermon, exhortation or meditation.

More and more I discovered that I was able to watch the service run itself. Sometimes I found myself sitting in the congregation instead of at the vicar's prayer desk, or accepting an invitation to lead a service in another parish, while the laity took charge of the Family Service without my supervision or intervention!

Extension

Having designed *Come and Worship!* for one particular situation, I discovered that this liturgical form had other varied uses in addition to providing a structure for Family Services.

I have found myself being invited to conduct 'prayers' in a range of situations and have wondered how best to fulfil this request. For example, I have been invited into guide camps and asked to lead worship on a Sunday evening. My response has been to suggest to the guides how we can work on a project to prepare for the Ministry of the Word together. We have then discovered how *Come and Worship!* gives a liturgical structure to the theme of our project.

I have also found *Come and Worship!* a helpful form of service to use in a house group of older teenagers. On some occasions the group has met to celebrate a house eucharist; on other occasions we have included in our evening meeting the related non-eucharistic liturgy of *Come and Worship!* Among a completely different group, when invited to lead prayers at the Mothers' Union I have felt on occasions the structure of *Come and Worship!* to be more appropriate than the offices recommended for use!

In all of these contexts *Come and Worship!* is able to offer a firm link between the regular central eucharistic act of worship in the church on a Sunday and the range of occasions when a simpler, less formal and non-eucharistic form of service is required.

4 SMALL VILLAGES

Andrew Bowden

Context

In addition to my work as chaplain of the Royal Agricultural College and bishop's adviser on rural society, I am rector of all I survey from my parsonage in Coates: 40 square miles of glorious Cotswold country and five medieval churches. There is everything God gives here, except people. In the seven hamlets which make up the benefice there are less than one thousand people all told. One in four of my parishioners is over retirement age and children are thin on the ground.

The pastoral needs of each village are, of course, different. Coates, with a population of 290, is clearly divided between the very rich and the rural poor. Tarlton, with a population of 120, has a lot of second homes and no village life at all. Rodmarton and Culkerton are both estate villages of 100 inhabitants each, but of quite different characters. Hazleton musters only 30 people and most of the cottages are rented out to students from the agricultural college. Frampton Mansell and Sapperton both have populations of around 170; tradition has it that they took opposite sides in the civil war and they still find it difficult to work together.

These small parishes embrace a very wide social mix. There are a few farmers, a few farm workers and lots more who used to be farm workers but who now work in one of the neighbouring towns. There are retired (knighted) civil servants, captains of industry who commute to London three days a week, devotees of the countryside and conservation, and craftsmen who have deliberately rejected industrial society.

This very variety, which is in one sense a richness, presents a great liturgical problem. For how do you provide satisfactory services for those who live and speak in the world of Shakespeare, for Coronation Street addicts and for disco devotees, all at the same time, particularly when on any one Sunday there will be no more than fifteen of them in church anyway?

To make sense of the situation, I have come to recognise that the village church needs to be able to minister to two quite different groups of people. On the one hand, there are the 'regulars' who are committed and attend most services. These are the people who keep the village churches going. The chief characteristic of the regulars is determination: what spurs them on is duty. Just like farming or gardening, their religion has its own rhythm and its own reward. So they feel that they need a liturgy which is regular and rhythmical, the weekly meal to keep up their strength along the pilgrim way.

On the other hand, there are the 'occasionals' who still very much want the village churches to be there, but whose expectations and commitment are not those of the regulars. The occasionals are a strange mixture of those who remember the 'old services' and like to hear again the echoes of their youth and those who know nothing of the church's liturgy. Both groups, however, have been conditioned by the media to respond to warmth, gentle humour and a variety of presentation. They want a service to be a celebration, a good entertainment in the best sense of the word; they want something that moves them and keeps alive in their hard old secular hearts the 'rumour of God'.

Since the liturgical needs of the occasionals are quite different from the liturgical needs of the regulars, the village church has to be able to offer two different kinds of services: a regular pattern for the regulars, but something quite different and rather special for the occasionals.

The regulars

The regulars will actually put up with anything, but there is no need for the regular service in a small village church to be quite as unwelcoming as it often is, or quite as off-putting to the occasionals who come along by chance. In his book *Rural Anglicanism*, Leslie Francis records the impressions of ordinands who arrived as occasionals at village services. Things which made these visitors feel uncomfortable included the clergy rushing in late, cold buildings, poor music, unfriendliness and lack of provision for children and young people. These are all problems which ring true to the country priest and which need to be ironed out.

The priest who is scheduled to conduct services at 8.30, 9.45 and 11.00 a.m. in three churches, some miles apart, is going to be in a rush. We have found that this need not be a real problem, provided that local people are responsible for switching on the lights and heating, getting the organist happy, organising the hymn board, checking that the lesson readers have turned up, making sure that books are open at the right place on the vicar's stall, and even beginning the service themselves so that the priest can slip in unobtrusively a few minutes late, if that is really necessary.

During the winter months, and sometimes well into spring, the small congregation cannot afford the luxury of heating a reasonably sized medieval church. Yet, I am sure that there is spiritual value in being warm on a February morning. My own experience is that the regulars are prepared, given certain assurances, to sacrifice 'my pew' on the altar of comfort. They will move up into the warm chancel. It should be one of our long term aims to establish a part of the church where the regulars can meet in warmth during the cold months, but in such a way that the area can be opened up again on the big occasions when we need to use the whole building.

Music modelled on Westminster Abbey is not always appropriate in the village church, sung by geriatric lungs and accompanied by a worn out organist. Where there is no regular choir to lead the music, we have decided not to sing the Anglican chants, let alone Merbecke's setting of the communion. Instead, we let the words of the psalms sing for themselves. Having no potential choir leader at present, we have resisted the temptation to try to restart the robed choir. Instead, we borrow those semi-professional choirs of enthusiastic adults, run by a good musician, who enjoy coming to a village church for a festival service.

The 'friendliness' of the village church is something quite different from the suburban church. On the one hand, in the village everyone knows everyone else, at least by sight and by reputation. On the other hand, lurking behind the countryman's outward friendliness is a deep reserve which defends him from hothouse familiarity in a narrow room. These people need to live alongside each other seven days a week, not just for an hour on Sunday. Formality is a necessary evil of the village, which often deeply affects the regular churchgoers. For this reason, I seriously doubt whether the 'kiss of peace' is either necessary or appropriate on the Sundays when the regulars meet together for worship.

What I am quite sold on, however, is the cup of coffee after the service. It is sometimes said that everyone sees each other so often that there is no need for a chat over coffee. Yet, in the modern village, this is not necessarily so. People need an excuse to do more than pass the time of day; the cup of coffee around the font is a wonderful way of integrating the locals and the newcomers, the young and the old, the regulars and the occasional churchgoers.

Probably the biggest challenge posed by the regular worship of the small village church concerns the place of children and young people. One of the saddest things I ever heard was said by a good young priest who had just moved with his family from a thriving town parish to a small village. He said, "I don't want my children to worship at our church; the services are so ghastly". And most of us must admit that our regular village services, compared to the thriving suburban scene, are 'unworthy' of children. Yet what we do have, if we will use them, is enough adults to take a close personal interest in every single child who comes and the very real opportunity of actively involving all our regular children and young people in the service itself, through serving, the offertory procession, lesson reading, bell ringing and so on.

This is a valuable start towards the small church's ministry towards children and young people, but clearly there is more to be done. In a sense, the children and young people are mid-way between the regulars and the occasionals. They are on the bridge, and also they are the bridge which makes it possible for us to link the two groups.

Children and young people

Small village churches, with populations between 30 and 300, are unlikely to achieve a great deal of successful work among children and young people unless they find ways of co-operating in larger units. Perhaps largely for historical reasons, village churches do not seem to find it easy to work together.

The five parishes in my benefice were not brought together with one clergyman until 1977. My poor predecessor had quite a hard time of it. As one villager put it, "He didn't want us and we didn't want him". By the time I was inducted in 1979, the worst of the hatchet work was done. Three years later, when the parishes realised that I was not going to close down any of the churches or even force the different communities to worship together, they actually volunteered that it would be a good thing to do together what none of them had the resources to do separately, namely work among children. They also recognised that the energy and commitment needed to come from the church members themselves.

It was in fact Wendy's initiative which brought together a group of parents and adults to start the Link Club. Some years earlier Wendy had tried to organise a Sunday school and failed. What made her new venture successful was the help she received from three or four other adults with skills which complemented her own, as well as a much wider pool of young people on which to draw. The Link Club, held just once a month in one of the village halls, brings in thirty or so children between the ages of four and eleven. Perhaps there is nothing very revolutionary in what goes on in the Link Club; the miracle is that it goes on at all.

The success of the Link Club spilled over into the foundation of a Sunday school run by Jill and her helpers. The Sunday school operates during school term in the school at Sapperton at the same time as the morning church service. This has been made possible by the interest and co-operation of the headteacher and the school cleaner. Inevitably, this Sunday school draws mainly from Sapperton itself, but a few children also come in from the other parishes. Now between ten and twenty children come into the second half of the morning service. They bring a feeling of lightness and joy into the church with them as they paddle up the aisle; even Sir Giles Poole, on his Jacobean tomb, smiles as they arrive.

In the other direction age wise, the Link Club spawned a youth fellowship for teenagers run by students from the local agricultural college. This happens in Coates during the college's term time only. Again, the youth fellowship works best among the young people who live in Coates, but two or three come in from the other parishes.

It is this work among children and young people which has occupied the central position in our strategy to cater for the liturgical needs of the occasionals.

The occasionals

Right from the start, I adopted the principle of having one service once a month in each major church designed to cater for the occasionals, those people on the fringes of the life of the local church who are not interested in becoming weekly churchgoers, but who respond to the invitation that the local church is doing something special and making a special effort to involve them. At Coates and Sapperton we adopted the Rite B Ministry of the Sacrament, following a completely informal Ministry of the Word. At Rodmarton we adopted a non-eucharistic Family Service. This pattern was well received and the children's joy and enthusiasm soon broke down any reservations about 'gimmickry' in church.

Since those early days, experience has taught us two important things about a regular pattern of services for the occasionals. First, such services depend on local enthusiasm and without 'local worship groups' they just do not work. The occasionals, children and adults alike, do not easily remember a monthly pattern of worship. They need to be reminded locally; they need to be regularly invited to take part; they need to be actively involved in the services and given the opportunity for responsible initiatives. So now we have local worship groups which take responsibility for sharing the planning of the family services in their villages and help to keep these services in the minds of their friends and neighbours.

Second, we learnt that Sunday morning at 9.15 a.m., the time when Coates is scheduled into my weekly itinerary, is too early for occasional families. Instead we have made a list of six times in the year when occasionals are encouraged to come. Three of these are school services, held in fact on weekdays, and three are at 3.00 p.m. on a Sunday afternoon.

The Link Club, Sunday school and family services are all drawn together by concentrating on a common theme. In addition, I am able to teach regularly in the three schools in my benefice and once again I concentrate on different aspects of the common theme. Thus, the family service is able to draw together what the children have been doing over the past month in school, Sunday school and Link Club and to share this with their parents and other adults.

There is a danger, of course, that by concentrating so much on material generated by children and young people that the family services might become 'child-worthy' only at the expense of ceasing to be 'adult-worthy'. We try very hard to avoid this pitfall by involving adults as much as possible in the preparation as well. A recent example of what we have in mind is given by the All Saints' festival at St Kenelm's, Sapperton.

All Saints at St Kenelm's

All Saints is a wonderful Christian feast, but it all remains locked away in the stained glass of Burne-Jones or William Morris unless we anchor it in 'the communion of saints' which we experience in our Christian pilgrimage. In other words, All Saints' tide is a prompt to thank God from the bottom of our hearts for those people, living and departed, whom we have known and who have showed us the meaning of love, uprightness and the faith of the Christian community.

All Saints is also an appropriate time for a village community to recollect its present identity with its own past. You cannot walk down a village street without seeing and touching walls and houses built by our ancestors. You cannot look over the hedges or dry stone walls into the neighbouring fields without recognising a landscape which our ancestors created by the sweat of their brow. You cannot walk through the churchyard into the village church without pondering the burial place of many previous generations and admiring the stone walls erected by our forebears to the glory of their God and to the glory of our God. The very village environment itself is the key resource for the celebration of All Saints' tide. The theme is as real for the adults in the village as for the children.

During October at school, Sunday school and the Link Club we gradually built up a project leading to the celebration of the Sunday following All Saints' day. We studied ancestors in the village, as a form of local history; we discussed our personal ancestors, as a form of family history; we explored the ancestors of the church, as an introduction to the saints; we began to tackle questions of death, dying and the communion of saints. This last theme may seem difficult, but, in the right context, the children were bubbling over to talk about what happens to us when we die —and what happens to our pets when they die!

The school and Sunday school contributed pictures and models to the family service. However, on this occasion, it was the Link Club which stole the centre of the stage by producing a splendid eight foot collage in milk bottle tops and other shiny materials, showing David as one of the Old Testament forerunners of the Christian church. Their collage of David presided over the family service, as a larger than life reminder of the roots from which today's church has emerged.

What made this theme particularly exciting for the whole community was the involvement of the schools. The headteacher at Sapperton is a wonderful teacher of local history; she is also an inspired producer of children's drama. No sooner had I begun to explore with her the theme of the All Saints' celebration than she had begun to evolve a pageant in homage of our village ancestors. The development of this pageant embraced many aspects of the school curriculum and at the same time caught the imagination and interest of the wider local community.

At the All Saints' tide Family Communion, the opening prayers were followed by a visual representation of significant features from the history of the local church and community: our patron saint, St Kenelm, being murdered by his sister whose eyes later dropped out; the merchants who brought salt down the ancient salt-way running at the top of the village; the yeomen who marked out our fields and built our houses; the local gentry who fought on opposite sides for king and parliament in the civil war; the carpenters and architects who settled in the village in the early 1900s and reconstructed our buildings as we now know them.

By the breadth of its historical perspective, this pageant visually cut us down to size, confirmed us in our historical roots and put us firmly in our eternal context. It led on naturally to our intercessions, when we remembered by name those who had died in the village during the last year. Our conventional communion service from *The Alternative Service Book 1980* somehow did not seem so conventional on this occasion, as we rejoiced 'with angels and archangels, and with all the company of heaven' to worship the God who chose to live in a village community.

The children who took part are unlikely to forget that All Saints' tide at St Kenelm's; nor are the adults likely to forget. That festival brought together young and old, occasional churchgoers and the regulars for the celebration of communion in their parish church. We had indeed built a bridge between the occasionals and the regular liturgy of their parish church, by articulating the felt need of the community to worship God through gratitude for our inheritance. We concluded the service with a prayer which seemed to sum up all our experiences:

We remember before you, O Lord,
those who brought us into the world,
    counselled us and guided us;
those who have borne with us,
    surrounded us with their influence and loved us;
those who laid out the fields,
    marked out the farms and cleared the ditches;
those who established our villages,
    built our churches and brought us the gospel of Christ.
Encourage us by their examples;
strengthen us by their fellowship
and count us, with them, among the saints in light;
through Jesus Christ our Lord.
Amen

5 LARGE CHURCHES

John Duckett

Context

I served my junior curacy in Boston, Lincolnshire, at the parish of St Botolph and St Christopher. Boston is a typical market town. For all its modest size, with a mere 25,000 inhabitants, it lords it over its own fenland kingdom. Indeed, you would have to go more than thirty miles to find a bigger town. Of those 25,000 inhabitants, 12,000 are in the parish of St Botolph and St Christopher. The parish comprises the commercial and industrial parts of the town, Victorian and Edwardian suburbs and modern housing estates, but not the posh suburbs.

The parish has two churches. St Botolph's is the cathedral-sized 'Boston Stump', a gigantic leftover from the middle ages, which makes the sky-scape of Boston so distinctive. St Christopher's, by way of a complete contrast, is a humble daughter church on a housing estate, no more than a simple wooden hut.

By the time I came to the parish, a monthly Family Service was well established, thanks to the pioneering work of the vicar, the Reverend Canon Trevor Collins, and the senior curate (known as the lecturer at Boston), the Reverend Dr Kenneth Stevenson. There had been many difficulties to overcome in order to establish the monthly Family Service, including the inhibitory size of the parish church and the opposition of those who felt that the Stump ought to stick to an 'establishment' style of worship, characterised by *The Book of Common Prayer* and the Anglican choral tradition. There was also the need to design services which would be flexible enough for use both at St Botolph's and at the very different St Christopher's on the succeeding Sunday. These problems could only be overcome if everybody worked together and the difficulties were properly talked out. The Family Service was, therefore, launched only after careful consultation and preparation.

I was immediately attracted to these services for several

reasons. They were adventurous and 'different'. They involved lay people in their planning and execution. They attracted people to the congregation who would normally never think of coming. Above all, they brought in the children; and once the children were there, the church came alive. As the vicar was fond of saying, and on impeccable gospel grounds too, it is not the children who need us; it is we who need the children.

Space

I think that one of the secrets of the success of Family Services at the Stump was that the size of the church was treated as an asset instead of a liability. For a start, it forced us to plan our services properly and to rehearse them beforehand. There were too many people involved, clergy, choir, servers, Sunday school and so on, to leave anything to chance. Any uncertainties are crudely exposed in a big church, where you cannot rely on whispered messages or the vicar's improvisation.

Second, the size of the church forced us to think big. The one thing our church had lots of was space, naturally enough since it was orginally built for grand processions and civic pomp. Consequently we learnt the value of mobility. I remember, among many other occasions, a Christmas procession when all the children were dressed as shepherds, and angels, and kings, and Josephs and Marys (for why should only one pretty girl be Mary?) filling the whole church with their pageant. On another occasion, the children pushed a large raft, on wheels and bearing a tall mast and sail, up the centre aisle, singing together as they pushed.

The effect was even more dramatic when the congregation was mobile too. For example, in a Family Service we called 'Stepping Stones' the whole congregation moved from the font, reminding us of the sacrament of baptism, to the chancel arch, symbolising for us the sacrament of confirmation, and then to the altar, focusing our attention on the sacrament of communion. At each station we celebrated the stages of our growth in discipleship.

Always we had to go for big, sweeping effects. It was no use, for instance, a child holding up his or her picture for us to see.

Beyond the tenth pew back, a normal size picture would seem no bigger than a postage stamp. So children's artwork had to be magnified into posters, friezes or banners, done with large paint-brushes or giant crayons. They had to be held up by a group of children, standing on chairs, not just by an individual child.

Drama, too, had to be larger than life. Carefully rehearsed mime with exaggerated gesture was the norm. In designing drama, dialogue had to be minimal, otherwise, given that we had to use a public address system to amplify the sound, a play would easily degenerate into a game of 'pass the parcel' in which everybody would be wondering which of the children would be first to drop the microphone.

We found it useful on occasions to work in duplicate or triplicate, rather like the stewards and stewardesses rehearsing the safety routine for the passengers on a large aeroplane. For instance, in a carefully rehearsed demonstration of making the Christmas pudding during an Advent service, we had three 'mums' and their families, placed at intervals down the central aisle. It sounded a hubbub from the chancel step, but the congregation apparently found it easy enough to tune into the nearest group.

Similarly, when children have prepared small pictures or models for a Family Service, the same kind of technique can be used. Instead of asking one child to display his or her work at the front of the church, several children can be asked to display their contributions at different points throughout the whole church.

Equipment

If large medieval churches are to be used effectively for contemporary Family Services, careful thought needs to be given to seeing that they are adequately equipped with appropriate communication aids. Often the purchase of high quality equipment is negligible in comparison with the cost of maintaining the medieval fabric itself.

To begin with, in a large church, you must make good use of sound effects. In order to do this well, you need a really good public address system and must be prepared to pay for it. Ideally such a system involves a set of speakers acoustically designed to match the needs of the building, a versatile system of micro-phones, cassette and record decks, adequate amplifiers and mixers. Our public address system at the Stump was excellent, so we were able to use music, recorded dialogue and sound effects as part of our worship.

Similarly, a large church gives good opportunity for the use of lighting effects. We were rarely able to exploit the full possibilities of our spotlights at the monthly Family Service, because this was held at ten o'clock in the morning. However, the occasional special evening service, at Christmas for instance, was enough to show how a mime or procession, given the right lighting, can in a large church be positively spectacular.

We also considered it important to make attractive service booklets for each service. Town churches should usually have the resources to do this. At the Stump we had a very efficient part-time secretary and a good duplicating machine. Our booklets were designed to make the structure of the service clear: they provided for congregational responses in the liturgy and they made a worthwhile memento to take away after the service.

Forgiveness

If these, then, were our methods of presentation; what of the actual content of the services? Given the limitations of space I have chosen to describe just one Family Service and I have selected this particular service because it has the flexibility to be mounted, given the necessary changes, in either a big or a small church. This example also demonstrates how our Family Services tried to be faithful to the liturgical structure both of the eucharist and of the lectionary. The service which I shall describe was held on the seventh Sunday after Pentecost, where the lectionary theme in *The Alternative Service Book 1980*'s cycle of readings is described as 'the most excellent way'.

The essential message of this lectionary theme concerns the forgiveness of God and how we in turn ought to forgive other people. In the light of this theme we decided to highlight key sections of the first part of the communion service itself. The collect naturally summed up the message of the service. The gospel reading illustrated the theme in the teaching of Jesus himself. The penitential sections, including the kyrie, confession and absolution, involved us all directly in the personal drama of the recognition of sin and of the experience of God's forgiveness.

For the ministry of the word, it was tempting to dramatise the day's gospel, the story of the unforgiving servant from Matthew's gospel, chapter 18. However, an oblique approach is often more helpful to the adults, particularly those for whom the story is staled by familiarity. We eventually found a suitable alternative approach, stimulated by an idea in the book *Share the Word* published by CIO. This was the story of the ink-blot. The story tells how Johnny literally blotted his copybook and what his teacher did about it. This idea was attractive because anything to do with school touches an emotional chord in most of us, since we have all been through that particular mill, whether we remember it with pleasure or with pain. Having identified the ideas and images suggested by this story, we set out to find the appropriate resources. Useful props turned out to be an ancient inkwell and dip pen, borrowed from the church vestry, and an old fashioned school desk, borrowed from the rectory.

The service began with a dramatised telling of the story. Johnny had just been given a *new* exercise book (can you remember how exciting that always was at your primary school?) and then had promptly spilt ink on its centre pages. All the other children of course went "Ummm!" And so what will the teacher do? They all waited to see. She could have been very cross ("You stupid boy ..."), she could have punished him ("You spoilt that book, and now you will be punished for it") or she could have made him look silly in front of the others ("Isn't Johnny a stupid, clumsy boy? Just look at him everybody").

In fact, the teacher did none of these things. Because she saw Johnny was sorry, she gave him a second chance. She accepted the blot Johnny had made and began to create something beautiful out of his mistake. After adding another blot or two, folding the pages and pressing them together, she opened the book up to reveal a symmetrical butterfly-shape. The other children were delighted and wanted to make one too. Johnny was very grateful to the teacher.

Here we invited the children to come out and to make some blot pictures too, the brushes, paint and pots of watercolour all having been prepared in readiness. They blobbed colours on the paper, folded the paper, pressed it, opened it out again and then showed the congregation what they had made.

The ministry of the word was concluded by reflecting on how this illustration of the ink-blot illuminates the character of God's own forgiveness. If we are truly sorry, then God can even use our mistakes and failures for good, to help us to become more beautiful in our living and to make our relationship with him deeper and more thankful. The gospel for the day, Jesus' own story about forgiveness until 'seventy times seven', was then read.

After the ministry of the word, the prayers were focused around the theme of penitence. The intercessions for others included prayers for the people whom we find it hard to forgive. The collect of the day was used, out of its usual sequence, to bring the central theme back sharply into focus. We finished with the prayer 'Lord, make us instruments of your peace'.

The peace was passed at this service with the special intention of signalling acceptance and forgiveness among the worshipping community, after a short explanation of why this is done. Then in the offertory procession the children brought out their own ink-blot pictures. The president placed these pictures on the altar and explained how at the eucharist we offer ourselves, complete with our ink-blots and stains, and ask God to take us just as we are, to use us in his service and to transform us into something beautiful for himself. The offertory hymn needed to say just the right thing to accompany this action; what we finally chose was 'Amazing Grace'.

The theme of the service was, of course, completed and brought to its climax by the communion itself.

Conclusion

During my time at Boston I came to formulate three main conclusions about Family Services, conclusions which I still find equally valid now that I am working in smaller churches.

First, I conclude that Family Services should have their theme set by the lectionary, so that they form an integral part of the weekly rhythm of the worship and teaching programme for the church. Otherwise there will always be the temptation at planning sessions to choose themes with a high entertainment value, which means that we shall fail to present a rounded gospel.

Second, I conclude that there is a natural place for the celebration of the eucharist at the heart of Family Services. The eucharist is the family meal of the church; it is, therefore, the prototypical Family Service anyway. The communion is simply the natural climax to the Family Service. If it is a 'good' Family Service, then the communion will have been deepened and illuminated for us all in some fresh way. That, for me, is the test of whether or not it has been worthwhile worship.

And lastly, I believe that in planning Family Services, we should always have in mind the old Chinese proverb:

I hear and I forget,
I see and I remember,
I do and I understand.

6 FRIDAY CLUB

Paddy Phillips

Context

Limber is a village of less than 300 people, with a pond, a primary school for thirty children, a pub, a shop and a seven hundred year old church. Most of the men work on the farms or in the estate departments around the village; families often settle for many years, becoming the backbone of the stable and remarkably self-contained community.

There are disadvantages to this seemingly ideal pastoral scene. Being self-contained we do not look often enough outside our own confines and could with ease become isolated and introverted. Being such a small community, human resources are limited and over-stretched. For example, on a 'bad' Sunday there are more people in the church choir than in the congregation, leaving the younger children, whose parents are the choir, too thickly and unsatisfactorily spread among the remaining congregation.

Limber church is part of a group of four parishes, sharing one priest. This means that the Sunday service pattern is irregular. On the second and fourth Sundays in the month there is a morning Family Communion in Limber at 11 o'clock. On the first and third Sundays the main service is Evensong at 6 o'clock. There is also the monthly 8 o'clock Holy Communion on the first Sunday in the month. Sunday school used to take place in church at 11 o'clock on those Sundays when there was no mid-morning service in Limber.

This irregular pattern of services led to confusion for the children, who were never quite sure whether it was 'Church Sunday', a Sunday usually to be avoided, or Sunday school. It also meant that teachers were unable to join in worship happening at other churches within the group, even if they wanted to. For many farm working families Sunday is their only day off and Sunday school, therefore, is low on their list of priorities.

Fridays

Against this background and a lot of raised eyebrows, we decided to change Sunday school from Sunday morning to Friday evening, immediately after school, from 3.30 to 4.30 p.m. We decided to meet in the vicarage which is only a short distance from the school. The results of this change from Sunday to Friday have been interesting, encouraging and unexpected.

To begin with, the attitude of the children is quite different. They come not in their Sunday best, polished, brushed and subdued, but crushed and crumpled by their week at school, feeling free and uninhibited. They have just been let out of school for the weekend and there is a certain air of exuberance.

Second, all activities reflecting anything of formal school are out. The children's powers of concentration are limited by their tiredness, so our work has to be informal, free, light-hearted and very well prepared to be ready for them. Reading and writing produce a 'nil-return'. The change in time has been a contributory factor to bringing about a shift from teaching Anglican facts and bible stories to becoming a group of children and adults more relaxed and more concerned with their relationships within the body of the church.

Third, more children come on a Friday than came on a Sunday. They remind each other at school and more naturally drift along together. It has become a group activity: it is what the village children do after school on Friday. From the parents' point of view, mothers seem to enjoy an extra hour's shopping before the weekend and it is as easy to collect children from the vicarage as it is from the school. It does not impose extra organisation on the parents, like the organisation needed to get the children to Sunday school on a Sunday morning. Friday afternoon fits more naturally into the normal rhythm of the week.

Fourth, there is greater opportunity to build up personal relationships between children and adults. The teachers arrive early to prepare their work and are then ready to greet the children when they arrive. At this point they fulfil the rôle of parents, hearing and receiving the news of the day, soothing cut knees and hurt souls. The feelings of family and trust do increase. Our worship and prayer can and does reflect the happenings of the day and becomes real.

Fifth, the day school becomes more involved in the life of the church, as the children talk naturally about what they are going to be doing after school. Help and encouragement are given by the school and the child's life becomes more integrated. There is much less of a 'Church and God are what we do on Sundays' idea. God becomes much more part of everyday life.

Finally, both the teachers and children are free to join in Sunday worship with the rest of their own family and the wider family of the church. They even have the opportunity to attend Sunday services in the other churches within the group!

However, now that Sunday school is happening on a weekday, there is the danger that the children may not see the link between their Friday Club and the worship of the church. There has to be special thought given to making the children really feel part of the Sunday worshipping family, so that the children do not see Sunday school and church as unrelated activities. At the same time, the adult churchgoers have to be helped to accept the children as part of their community.

To forge this link between the children and the adult worshipping community, we have begun to sum up a month's work, or sometimes even a whole term's work, in worship at the Family Communion. This involves the children presenting the Ministry of the Word in some form, leading the prayers and taking responsibility for the readings. At the same time the children's creative work is displayed in the church. When the children are responsible for the worship, their behaviour in church improves a hundredfold, because they can see the point of it all.

Our village

To illustrate this link between the Friday Club and the Sunday morning Family Communion, I shall describe just one particular occasion. Last September we wanted to hold a Family Communion a few weeks before the parish's large Harvest Festival. By this time of year the corn harvest is already the main concern of the village. We needed to acknowledge that this was going on, but we did not wish in any sense to anticipate the theme of the Harvest Festival to be celebrated in just a few weeks' time.

We chose as the theme for the September Family Communion 'the body of Christ'. We wanted to make the point that the body of Christ, the family of God, is not restricted to Sunday school or to the church doing 'religious things'. Our theology tells us that God's family includes the whole village working community, as well as the worshipping community of the village church.

We began to prepare for the September Family Communion about six weeks in advance. The first step involved looking at the characteristics of the village and identifying the key people responsible for undertaking representative jobs in the community. We picked eight particular individuals: a farmer, a hairdresser, the vicar, the church cleaner, a gardener, a housewife, a gamekeeper and the blacksmith. We then asked these eight people if they would work alongside two children each for an hour and a half to two hours. We wanted the children to see something of their jobs and, if possible, to participate in the way they spent their time.

All this took considerable planning and explaining to get the right children alongside the right adults. One of the advantages of living in a small community is that the children at least know the faces of the adults and sometimes know them quite well. In this way fear of unknown adults was not a worry to them, or to their parents. After the initial arrangements had been made the children wrote invitations to their 'hosts' inviting them to come along to the September Family Communion with them, so that the project would culminate in us all worshipping together.

Before the children went on their visits, the Friday Club spent some time looking at and talking about our village, its people and their work. We discussed how each job and each person is important and how they each play an integral part in the life of the community. We looked at a map of the village and the church. We marked where each of us lived and saw that although we lived in individual families, together we were one community.

After the children had been on their visits, they recorded their experiences. They painted pictures of what they had discovered of the village and these pictures were displayed in church.

Two young mothers joined the group to help the children design and make a collage altar frontal, depicting the work in which they had been sharing. It is the practice at the Family Communion for our parish church not to use the main altar in the chancel, but to bring a simple hessian covered kitchen table into the nave. It is, therefore, comparatively easy to make a frontal with an extra piece of hessian and to fix it on to the front of the table with a trigger tacker. They used a wide range of collage materials to create a bold representative design, full of flowers and tractors, church and combine harvesters, and with big bold letters proclaiming 'We are the body of Christ'.

During the week before the September Family Communion the children prepared the church for the celebration. The two children who had worked alongside the church cleaner now joined her again to clean and polish the church. The two children who had worked alongside the gardener joined him again to choose flowers for the church and to help arrange them. Other children, working with the housewife, baked biscuits in the vicarage kitchen to share at the service.

For the service itself the children prepared and led the intercessions and thanksgivings, with special emphasis on the life and work of our own community. With the help of a guitar-playing father, the children led the singing of 'We are one in the Spirit, we are one in the Lord'. The children also took responsibility for the ministry of the word. They made good use of the collage altar frontal to talk about the people they had been working with and to illustrate their different work.

Through this service both the children of the Friday Club and the worshipping community of Limber church came to appreciate the significance of our interdependence in the village and how this illustrates our interdependence in the body of Christ. We each have our contribution to make and our gifts to give; at the same time we each have the need to receive from others.

Lent

Every so often our idea of summing up the work which we have been doing in the Friday Club at the Family Communion runs into a major problem. This year we wanted to make use of the sessions during Lent to prepare for Easter Sunday, but Easter Sunday happened to fall on one of those days when Limber only had a 6 o'clock evening service. Easter Sunday could not be changed; nor could the pattern of services in the parishes, because the vicar was needed in his other churches. We also knew that it was quite unrealistic to expect many Limber children to travel to the Family Communion services at the other churches in the group of parishes. We decided, therefore, to focus our Friday Club sessions on preparing for a Family Service to be held on Good Friday. For good measure we also decided to hold an additional preparation session on Maundy Thursday.

During the sessions before Holy Week the Friday Club gave the children the opportunity to explore themes concerned with Jesus' preparation of the disciples for his death, the disciples' fear and the power of new life to overcome death. We broke eggs and used them for cooking, talking of the life within if the conditions are right for it to develop. We planted cress seeds in the broken egg shells and watched new life grow from seeming lifelessness. We sat in a circle, round a lighted candle, and learnt the song 'Out of darkness came light'.

On Maundy Thursday we met at 9.30 in the morning for a four-hour project. The regular members of the Friday Club were joined by some other children who cannot normally be with us after school on a Friday, like those who go away from the village for their schooling. The usual band of female helpers was joined by a sixteen year old boy who came along to play his guitar and by a man who had time and energy on his hands.

All the children met together for the first half hour. Badges were given out and the day was organised. We sang to the guitar and joined in opening prayers. Then we divided into three groups for the first session until 10.45 a.m. The four to six year olds made happy faces mobiles and Easter cards. The six to eight year olds collected wheelbarrows full of earth from a building site, causing much speculation in the village. Then they gathered grass and moss to make a green hill on a large board. The eight to twelve year olds made hot cross buns, while in between the various stages of the baking process they worked on two banners with collage materials, depicting 'Jesus is Alive' and 'out of darkness came light'.

After a fifteen minute break for drinks, the groups met for a second session between 11 and 12 o'clock. This time the four to six year olds produced a collage on the theme of 'new life'. The six to eight year olds made wooden crosses for the green hill and busied themselves on a treasure trail. The eight to twelve year olds continued baking hot cross buns and making their collage banners.

Our shared lunch at noon, round one very large table, was a gentle reminder of the way in which Jesus shared the last supper round the table with his disciples on that first Maundy Thursday.

Immediately after lunch we shared in some games together and then we all helped to carry the 'green hill' into church on its large wooden board. In church we looked at the screen with the large crucifix showing Jesus on the cross. Then we sang the hymn 'There is a green hill' and went home.

On Good Friday the 10 o'clock Family Service was a service of participation. We ate the hot cross buns made the day before; we made a procession of palms; we became the friendly crowd and shouted "Hosanna"; we became Judas going out of the church individually and alone; we gathered together as the hostile crowd and shouted "Crucify him"; we stood with our arms outstretched by a life-size cross until our arms ached. Before we left for home we sang 'Lord of the dance' by a bush shaped like an open tomb. We felt those events.

On Easter Saturday we came back to the church. We put up the banners we had made; we displayed the mobiles and the friezes. We even helped to decorate the church with flowers.

On Easter Sunday some Limber children travelled to another church in the group for the Family Communion, where they shared in the preparation made by another parish. Here a large hen had laid chocolate eggs in a basket during the service for the children as they went home. Other Limber children came to the evening service of 'Songs of Praise' in Limber church. In some senses we hardly noticed the fact that Limber had missed its Family Communion this Easter Sunday morning.

Conclusion

The change from the traditional Sunday school to the new Friday Club has been appreciated by the children, their parents and the Sunday school teachers. As well as attracting more children, it has fostered a greater feeling of family identity within the young people of the church and helped to build bridges between the children's everyday experiences and the life of the local church. These have been a real added bonus to the other practical advantages of having Sunday school on Friday.

While it was comparatively easy to change the time and content of the traditional Sunday school, it has not been possible to change its name. Now everyone in Limber speaks about Sunday school happening on Friday; it all adds to the fun.

7 FAMILY PROJECT DAY

Leslie J. Francis

Context

My first Family Project Day took place when I was priest-in-charge of two small parishes in Suffolk, Little Wratting and Great Bradley. Little Wratting and Great Bradley are at opposite ends of a valley, separated by Great Wratting, Great Thurlow, Little Thurlow and Little Bradley. The area was undergoing pastoral reorganisation. Each of the six parishes has its own medieval church, and together all six muster a total population of about 1,100. The Bradleys and Thurlows feed the Church of England controlled first school in Thurlow, while children from the Wrattings tend to go to first schools in Kedington and Haverhill.

The aim of the first Family Project Day was to see if all six parishes, and the three clergymen involved in their pastoral care, could work together to build a bridge between the churches and young people.

At the planning stage we sharpened our aims in a number of ways. We decided to major on work with five to eleven year olds, but also to include provision for teenagers. We recognised that we wanted to work both with young people who knew something about the church and sometimes came to services, as well as with young people who knew virtually nothing about the church and hardly ever came. We decided that what we needed to do was to spend a whole day, a Saturday, conducting project workshops with young people and using these workshops to prepare for a church service on the Sunday. This, we thought, would be the bridge between the child's learning and enjoyment and the regular worship of the church in these parishes. We decided that the Sunday service should be the modern form of communion used from time to time in the parishes, as set out in my children's communion book, *The Lord is Here!*

Next, we had to decide when to hold our first Family Project

Day. Lots of factors pointed to late September or very early October. The theme, then, was obvious: we would celebrate harvest.

Preparation

St Luke's parable about counting the cost before building a tower is an eminently sensible one. It seemed essential that the first Family Project Day should be such a success that it would lead on to future events. At first costing, the needs of the day far outstripped our apparent resources.

First of all we needed somewhere to hold the day. The rural church is desperately short of purpose-built, educationally designed, plant. In Great Wratting, where I lived, there was neither school nor church hall. The medieval church was by itself hardly suitable for a project day. But what did remain in the parish was one resource of inestimable worth: the diocese had not yet sold the Victorian rectory. I decided to put almost every room in my rectory at the disposal of the project, except my study and my bedroom. The stables and outhouses were smartened up for the occasion as well. Fortunately, the garden was quite large and butted onto the churchyard, so that the church could be regarded as all part of the same complex. The first resource problem was solved.

Second, we needed to review our human resources. We needed to enable the parishes to catch the vision and to realise that the resources were in fact available. But just in case this failed, I invited in two sources of help from outside. The diocesan religious education adviser offered to come to stay over the weekend and so did a handful of students from a Cambridge College Christian Union. We wanted the project to be generated from within the parishes, but we also wanted to make sure that there was a group of people who could help out if necessary. After several months of talking with parishioners, I realised that the second resource problem was also solved.

Months before the first Family Project Day, I began to spin my vision in conversation with individual people. "Are you interested?" I asked, "what can you do to help?" A wide range of offers began to trickle in.

Some offers came from people who were professionally used to working with children. A London art teacher who had a weekend cottage in one of the villages offered to run an art workshop. "In the morning," she said, "I will run a workshop for children. In the afternoon I will do something for their parents and for other adults." The headmistress of the village school offered her skills. Another teacher said that she did not think that it was fair to ask her to work with children on her day off, but that she would be willing to take care of writing the notices and organising the display of the finished work.

Other offers came from people skilled in particular ways. A professional carpenter offered to set up a woodwork workshop. A cook offered to set up a cooking workshop to bake bread. Someone whose hobbies included wine-making suggested making some home-made wine. A skilled needlewoman suggested a needlework workshop. One of the church organists offered to borrow percussion instruments from a local school to make music. Someone else suggested classes in making corn dollies. Other offers included dance, drama, craft skills and so on. My task was simply that of seeing how all these diverse offers could be co-ordinated into a sensible Saturday programme which would enrich the Sunday eucharist.

At more practical levels we also needed to plan additional toilet facilities, first aid provision, transport and parking. While we were concentrating on a project for five to eleven year olds, we recognised the need to arrange crèche facilities for the under fives. Finally, while our theology balked at the notion, practical constraints meant that we prayed for fine weather!

Project

When the Saturday eventually arrived, the sun shone (although in later years we learnt how to cope in rain and wind and cold!). Children, helpers and other adults began to arrive at the rectory soon after 10.00 a.m. They were greeted, given a name label, shown where to store their packed lunch and invited to walk around and to see 'what was on offer'.

Around the rectory garden there were notices advertising what was going to happen during the day and the helpers milled around freely to talk with the children about the different workshops. Then the church bell began to ring and we all made our way into the neighbouring church for a prompt 10.30 a.m. start.

As we arrived in church, we were immediately caught up in an atmosphere of guitar-led singing. There was no opportunity given to the children for them to become bored or restless! At 10.30 a.m. the singing stopped, the children and adults were given a brief warm welcome. They were told succinctly what the day was about. Then a candle was lighted at the chancel step and we watched it attentively for just one minute in complete silence, to focus our minds on God and on the activities of the day. Next the church door was opened. We rushed back to the rectory garden and each person joined one of five groups. Each group then went off site to see something and to do something as a way of establishing an experience on which the day could build.

All five groups did something which related to the harvest theme. A local landowner took a group of children to clamber over his combine harvester and to see the harvested fields. He gave them some sheaves of corn to bring back to the rectory. Someone who kept goats took a group to feed the goats and to milk them. She gave the children jugs of milk to bring back to the rectory. Another group went off to the hedgerows in one of the other parishes to look for blackberries. They came back with their plastic bags full. The churchwarden took a group home to his orchard and invited them to share in his harvest of apples. They returned with their baskets full. The fifth group piled into cars to drive off to a nearby windmill, where they saw how corn used to be turned into flour. They, too, came back with some corn.

As the groups returned to the rectory, the children sorted themselves out into a range of workshops. The corn collected from the farm needed grinding by the small hand-turned grinders; the ground flour needed mixing with yeast and the dough needed baking. A large part of the dough was used to bake ordinary loaves and rolls, while a group of teenagers used some of it to sculpture a special harvest loaf, in the shape of a sheaf of corn. The blackberries were to be turned into wine. The milk was to be put through a separator and then shaken for hours until it began to turn into butter. The apples were to be cooked and turned into pies. Soon the rectory was full of tempting cooking smells. Our five journeys had produced the essential gifts of bread and wine for the Sunday eucharist and the food for a snack after the service.

Those who came back from their field trip not wanting to bake bread, make wine or cook apples could use their energies in a number of other ways. Different workshops enabled them to build models, paint pictures, construct collages and attempt creative writing. Some of the boys began to make a large cardboard model of the combine harvester. A small group of girls began to build a model of the barn in which the combine harvester was stored. The art room became alive with scenes of ripening corn, bright suns shining above ancient windmills and colourful tractors. In another corner a whole model farm and road network was under construction.

Half past twelve saw a change in activity, as we settled down on the grass to eat our lunches. Clusters of adults and children were busy comparing the food they had brought with them and swapping sandwiches. After lunch we spent a short while playing games and organising a scavenger hunt. Then it was time for the afternoon workshops to begin.

Keith, who was responsible for the music workshop, walked round the garden playing a percussion instrument. Gradually he collected a group of children and adults who followed him into church. The music workshop created their own music for the offertory procession. At the same time, Margaret, who was responsible for the dance workshop, attracted a group of young teenagers to one of the attic rooms in the rectory. The dance workshop prepared a contribution for the ministry of the word.

Derek set up his woodwork workshop in the old stables and began to fashion, with his band of helpers, a processional cross and candle holders. Cheryl gathered around her a group of children to make the candles, heating the wax on a portable gas stove. Brin re-orientated her art workshop from children to adults. One or two teenagers settled down to creative writing. Vernon led a choral speaking group which was responsible for choosing the scripture readings and for arranging how they would be presented in the service by a number of voices.

At the same time, some of the workshops begun in the morning prepared for their second session of the day. John and Richard continued with their model-making workshop outside on the rectory lawn. Sandy continued with the collage which had taken over one of the rectory bedrooms. Another bedroom had become the home of the group making corn dollies. Margaret continued with her small group of adults and teenagers in the rectory dining-room, working on the special chasuble being fashioned for the Sunday service. Other adults floated between groups, keeping an eye on individual children and making sure that they were relating constructively to one group or another.

All too soon, we found ourselves having to wind down our diverse activities and to prepare for the end of the day. The day ended, as it began, in church. At four o'clock guitar-led singing began once again in the church and the church bell summoned us all back. Already some of the work had been assembled in the church and the children brought more of their work with them as they came in.

In church we spent a short while telling each other about our experiences and giving thanks to God. Then we went away, looking forward to returning to Sunday's harvest eucharist.

After the children and their parents had gone home, the real work seemed to begin. Now was the time to display the work in the church and to assess what had emerged by way of dance, music and speech. With the help of the students staying in the rectory, all these contributions were welded together with some drama as a coherent ministry of the word. Finally, some of the children's creative writings and line drawings were assembled with the scipture readings and hymns to produce a special service booklet. Somehow, the scanner and the duplicator seemed to be working late into the Saturday evening.

When Sunday came, the eucharist was celebrated around a portable table serving as a nave altar, and even the sanctuary was needed to provide space for an overflowing congregation.

The service began with a procession, headed by Derek's wooden cross and Sandy's collage banner. The extended ministry of the word enabled the congregation to share in Saturday's fun. The voice of scripture, orchestrated by Vernon's choral reading workshop, came from the four corners of the church. The visiting students re-enacted the message of the gospel in drama and led into Margaret's liturgical dance group.

The offertory procession was accompanied by Keith's percussion music. Home-made candles were brought to the nave altar, together with one of the loaves we had baked the previous day. The wine to be used in the communion was brought up alongside the blackberry juice which had just begun its fermentation process. Examples of our various craft work were also placed around the altar.

After the service the congregation were invited to stay and try some of our other harvest baking: bread spread with butter made from the goat's milk and apple pies. Children and adults lingered to look at the work displayed in the church and to tell each other about their part in the Family Project Day.

Conclusion

We discovered that what had begun ostensibly as an attempt to work with five to eleven year olds had in fact achieved so much more. A great deal of interest, enthusiasm and hard work had been released from people of all ages; and all this had been offered to God in the eucharist.

As a consequence of this experience, the Family Project Day became an established part of the harvest celebrations for several years. We also 'tried similar events for Christmas, Easter and Whitsun. A good Family Project Day requires a great deal of energy and time to be invested in planning and preparation. We discovered that we had the resources to mount one or two good Family Project Days in a year, but certainly no more. In retrospect, one good Project Day a year is probably enough to achieve the objectives of focusing the skills and energies of the community into the celebration of eucharist and of showing that a real bridge can be built between the life of the worshipping community and the interests of secular children.

8 GOOD FRIDAY PROJECT

Doreen Storr

Context

Louth is a market town of some 13,000 people. Louth Parish is a team ministry: a team rector and two team vicars serve the three town churches and three neighbouring village churches. At the moment the team is in the happy position of having a curate. The three town churches offer a range of churchmanship, varying from high church to evangelical. The three village churches also embrace a variety of traditions.

Although each church has tended to carry on its own children's work independently of the others, there have been two important ways in which the churches have worked together in this area. First, the teachers themselves have met for many years to share ideas, to plan and to work together. Second, there is now a well-established history of the churches co-operating to plan a joint summer adventure day for the children of the whole parish. This adventure day has moved around the various churches; the location has included a farm in a country parish, a large house in the town, and a church controlled school. Against this background of co-operation, we decided to try to arrange a joint event for Good Friday.

In previous years Family Services have been held in some of the town churches on Good Friday. Experience had shown, however, that these Family Services were failing to meet the needs of either the children or their parents. Good Friday is an especially difficult occasion to structure all-age worship. The kind of compromises offered seemed either to deprive the adults of the unique spiritual discipline of Good Friday or to offer the children something with which they had difficulty identifying.

This year, therefore, we decided to try to offer something on Good Friday specifically for pre-teenage children, in which they could participate at their own level, leaving their parents free to participate in the more traditional Good Friday liturgy. In planning a Good Friday Project for children we had three particular aims in mind. First, we wanted to give the children the opportunity to prepare something which they could share with the whole worshipping community during the Eastertide services in church. Second, we wanted them to be able to make something they could take home to share with their families and through which they could explore the significance and meaning of Easter. Third, we wanted to enable them to enter into the spiritual atmosphere of Good Friday itself.

Preparation

Preparation started in January, when Good Friday still seemed a long way off. If our Good Friday Project was going to be a success, plans needed to be formed well in advance.

Timing was the first consideration so that the children's Good Friday Project would fit in with the other services in the parish. We decided to plan a three-hour project to coincide with the traditional three hours devotion from 12 noon until 3 o'clock. This would enable parents to attend the service in church if they so wished. It would also free the children and their leaders to join with the church congregation and with other parishioners, after the three-hour project, to take part in the Good Friday procession of witness through the streets of the town.

The next thing to consider was what form the children's three-hour project should take. We decided that the three hours would be divided up between times of activity and times of quietness and worship. The activity periods would enable the children both to prepare something for the Eastertide services in church and to make something to take home and share with their families. The times of quietness and worship would enable them to enter into the spiritual experience of Good Friday. We were also keen to see lunch together as an integral part of the day.

It is always difficult to guess what kind of response there is going to be for something new in a parish. We hoped that the day might attract at least thirty children, so we needed to plan the activity periods and the worship sessions accordingly. We decided that it would be good to meet together in one group for the worship and for lunch, but to divide up into several parallel groups for the activity periods. In this way the children would have the experience of being together as a whole group for worship and for eating, but also the chance to work in much smaller units on specific tasks.

When the shape of the day was worked out in greater detail, we planned three activity periods of thirty-five minutes each, three worship sessions of ten minutes each and a lunch time of forty minutes. Our programme looked like this:

12.00 p.m.	Introduction
12.05 p.m.	Group activities 1
12.40 p.m.	First worship session
12.50 p.m.	Lunch
1.30 p.m.	Group activities 2
2.05 p.m.	Second worship session
2.15 p.m.	Group activities 3
2.50 p.m.	Final worship session
3.00 p.m.	Finish

Such a firm timetable meant that disciplined organisation was very necessary so that the children could move smoothly between small group activities and corporate worship sessions.

Having decided on the shape of the three-hour project, we needed to take into account the facilities which the parish could offer. Fortunately St Michael's hall offered the ideal environment. There is sufficient space here for a range of activities to be allocated a room of their own. A comfortable carpeted room was set aside for the worship sessions. The main hall provided the right setting for lunch, and three or four separate rooms were available for the individual activities.

Three people volunteered to take charge of different activities. Each would run the same activity three times during the course of the day so that every child could have a go at all three activities, but not all at the same time! The children would move from group to group for each activity period.

One activity group would work on a collage of the events of Holy Week. This would enable the children to express their interpretation of the biblical narrative and to share their interpretation with the whole worshipping community by displaying the finished collage in one of the churches. The second group would work on individual Easter gardens, while the third group would use the kitchen to bake, making chocolate Easter nests. Both the gardens and the nests are powerful symbols through which the children could explore the Easter gospel of new life; and they could take their finished gardens and nests home with them. They would also take away with them a bookmark showing a cross to act as a permanent reminder of the day.

The three leaders who took charge of the activities then had the responsibility of enlisting others to help them. Some of the helpers were recruited from among the Sunday school teachers, while others were people willing to give time on this specific occasion. Often church members who would never dream of teaching in a Sunday school are delighted to help children prepare collages and bake. Each leader was responsible for acquiring materials for the group, with expenses being met by the parish.

The worship sessions were my responsibility. I decided to centre the worship on the cross, building up the events of Holy Week and ending with Easter Sunday. I arranged the carpeted room we had set aside for worship so that the focus of attention would be a simple low table, with a large white cross pasted on a purple background to form a backcloth. There would be one candle in a holder to be lit at the last worship time, symbolising the risen Christ. The children would all sit on the floor and the signal for each time of worship would be music played on a cassette.

Another person volunteered to be responsible for preparing the main hall for lunch and to provide coffee and orange squash for the children and for the helpers.

Leaflets were printed advertising the day and distributed among the children associated with the six churches. The children or their parents were asked to fill in a tear-off slip and to return it before Good Friday, so that we should have some indication of the numbers likely to participate in the day.

By the time of the final planning meeting, a little before Good Friday, everything was already well in hand. What was important now was to anticipate the last minute problems, to make sure that we all understood the schedule and were willing to keep to it, and to encourage children to come.

Good Friday

We decided that it was wise to be at the church hall an hour and a half before the project was due to start. The worship room was set up and the areas set aside for the activities were allocated tables. These were covered with paper to protect them. The group leaders all arrived in good time and were able to set up their own areas. As well as the leaders providing their own materials, there was a central resource of scissors, felt-tip pens, glue and other basic equipment.

Children began to arrive about fifteen minutes before the starting time. They put their packed meals and their coats in the hall which was to be used for lunch and then came to sit in the carpeted room we had set aside for worship. They made their own groups, gathering their friends around them. By 12 o'clock thirty-eight children had arrived, making three groups of about a dozen each. Because the children formed their own groups from among their family and friends, these groups worked well together and all included a wide age range from four to twelve years.

At 12 noon the children were given a very brief outline of what was going to happen during the three hours. Then the group leaders took their groups and started the first activity period. The children got down to work very quickly and began to produce some attractive things.

In the first activity room, the children were making their individual Easter gardens in butter and margarine containers. Gravel and sand were used to form a basis for the gardens and a raised hill was made at one end. Crosses were made with wood and bound together with cotton to make the cross shapes. These were placed on the hill. The tomb was made from dough which had been prepared beforehand. This was very pliable and an ideal colour. Stones were used for the stone at the entrance to the tomb. Pieces of fir tree and forsythia which was just in bloom were used to give a good garden effect.

In the kitchen the Easter nests were made from shredded wheat and melted 'cake cover' chocolate. The children moulded this in paper case covers into a nest shape. The nests set fairly quickly and sugar eggs were placed in them. During the process the helpers were able to encourage the children to explore the significance of the nests as a symbol of the new life of Easter. A place was allocated in the kitchen for each groups' nests and the children's names were written on a piece of paper and placed under the paper cases. It is important that the children are able to take home what they have actually made themselves.

In the third activity room the children worked on the huge collage. Each activity period concentrated on its own individual picture so that each group of children would experience a sense of achievement when their own contribution was completed. At the same time, they knew that the three individual pictures would be brought together at the end of the project to create one large collage for display in the church. The first group worked on the Maundy Thursday scene on the Mount of Olives, with Jesus praying and the disciples sleeping. The second group took the Good Friday theme, showing the winding path leading to Calvary and the three crosses. In contrast to the rather sombre picture of Good Friday, the third group celebrated the joy of Easter Sunday with a riot of colour.

Each of the three worship sessions began in the same way by settling the children down to a short extract of 'theme music'. We chose 'Venus' from Gustav Holst's *The Planets* to help create a sense of peace and to establish the right mood for worship. Then the three sessions concentrated on the themes of Maundy Thursday, Good Friday and Easter Sunday in turn. Each session included looking at a picture which focused on the central images of the theme and drawing out from the children by question and answer the main events of the story. Towards the end of the session the picture was pasted onto the large white cross on the purple backcloth. A child read the account of the story from A.J. McCallen's book *Listen!*

Each of the three worship sessions ended in the same way with the recitation of the same prayer. In the first two sessions the prayer was said by the leader; in the final session the children were able to join in the prayer and to make it their own.

For the Good Friday story some of the curtains were drawn to dim the worship room. In sharp contrast the curtains were all drawn back and the light switched on for the Easter Sunday story. To mark the climax of the final session the candle was lit. Then, after the Easter Sunday picture had been fixed to the white cross, the backcloth was turned round to reveal a bright yellow background with a glittering gold cross on it. This cross was in the same design as the one the children were going to receive on their bookmarks to take home.

Conclusion

The three-hour Good Friday Project proved to be a very successful idea. It had enabled the children to focus on the events of Holy Week and Easter at their own level. It had also given parents the opportunity to spend some time on their own thinking about Good Friday and joining in with the parish worship. Time had gone very quickly and the children felt satisfied with their achievements. They had made things to take home and to share with their family and through which they could continue to explore the theme of the new life of Easter. At the same time, they had left their collage in church to share with the congregation on Easter Sunday.

9 TEDDY BEARS

Leslie J. Francis

Discovery

I suppose that teddy bears must always have been part of my congregation, but for the first five years or so of my ministry I completely failed to recognise their presence; and consequently I failed to minister to their spiritual needs. It was, first of all, Susan's bear who altered all that.

In the usual way I had been passing along the communion rail with the host. Susan's mother held out her hand to receive the bread and I pronounced the words of administration, "The body of Christ keep you in eternal life". Susan held her head high to be blessed and I placed my hands firmly on her hair and said, "Susan, the Lord bless you and keep you". Then suddenly Susan's bear raised his head. I was perplexed; ignoring the bear, I moved on to the next pair of outstretched hands, "The body of Christ keep you in eternal life". But as I stood there saying those words of administration, I became very conscious of a rather aggressive bear bashing and biting my ankles. A minute later Susan's bear was being projected across the sanctuary floor for all kneeling at the altar rail to see.

After the service, neither Susan nor her bear would speak to me or look at me. Later in the week Susan's mother began to help me to understand the strength and the power of the relationship which exists between the child and her bear. Of course, subconsciously I knew; I had been a child once and then I had been inseparable from my teddy bear, but it is so easy to forget what it is like to be a child. For Susan, her bear was no stuffed toy, not even an animal or a pet, but a real and living and very close friend. Psychologists would describe how the child projects onto the bear so many of her feelings, her hopes, her fears, her desires; indeed, so much of the child's developing psychological life can be lived out through the teddy bear. In rejecting Susan's bear I had, unwittingly, rejected Susan.

Following on from my conversation with Susan's mother, I had an equally long conversation with Susan and her bear. I said "Sorry" to bear, and I think bear said "Sorry" to me. Anyway, we seemed to part the best of friends. Next Sunday, as I passed along the altar rail, Susan held her head high as usual and this week so did her bear. After blessing Susan, I placed my hand firmly on the bear's head and said, "Rupert, the Lord bless you and keep you",.for having been introduced properly during the week I was now on Christian name terms with bear as well. And I suspect that, in blessing Rupert, the Lord extended his blessing to Susan by helping her feel more truly welcome in the eucharistic community of which she and her bear are essential parts.

While my discovery of the centrality of the teddy bear within the worshipping community took place in the context of the Family Communion, my colleague, John Gay, tells of his similar discovery in the context of the baptism service. John was conducting a baptism service for a three year old girl, Elizabeth. Elizabeth had seen the font filled with water. Parents and godparents had made their promises in her name. All was now ready for the baptism in water to take place.

As the moment of baptism drew closer, Elizabeth became more and more restive. She steadfastly refused to take an interest in the font and was determined to avoid getting wet at all costs. Her growing anxiety and insecurity were clearly expressed by the tight hold that she was keeping on her teddy bear.

At this point John decided to abandon the official liturgy for a while and to improvise. Forgetting parents and godparents, he talked directly with Elizabeth and soon found Elizabeth volunteering teddy to be baptised in her place. Solemnly taking teddy to the font, John asked Elizabeth to say his name. "Edward Bear", came the confident reply. Then John poured water on teddy's head and said "Edward Bear, I baptise you in the name of the Father and of the Son and of the Holy Spirit". Seeing how much teddy enjoyed being the centre of attention at the font, Elizabeth decided very happily that it was her turn next. What had begun for Elizabeth as a frightening and unhappy introduction to church was transformed by Edward Bear into an enjoyable and rewarding occasion.

Invitation

Having at last woken up to the fact that teddy bears were coming to church anyway, I decided that it was high time that my church should make a greater effort to help them feel really welcome. I talked with the headteacher of a local village school, a Church of England voluntary controlled first school, catering for forty children between the ages of five and nine. Together we decided to plan a Family Communion based on the theme of the teddy bears' picnic.

Over a period of almost half a term, the three classes in the school worked on a project preparing for the great picnic. To begin with, the music lessons began to teach John Bratton's 'The Teddy Bears' Picnic'. The simple and well known melody was soon supported by rhythmic percussion, tuned chime bars and recorders. Then various groups began to work on creating a huge collage backcloth depicting the woods where the picnic takes place. Bold brown tree trunks supported a riot of bare branches. Gradually the branches were brought to life with multicoloured leaves, birds, butterflies and squirrels. The undergrowth was transformed by bluebells, primroses, toadstools and hedgehogs. At first the collage was displayed in school and then it was tranferred to the church.

The top class set to work to prepare a short mime and dance. The thought of teddy bears dancing during the picnic suggested to them stiff movements and a plodding rhythm. Soon they began to devise their own costumes to go with the dance.

The children also began making their own teddy bears. Glove puppet teddies were based on papier mâché heads; simple cut out shapes were stuffed; some were even knitted. Pictures were painted of teddies and cut out to stick on every pew end.

Soon the children were discovering that teddy bears had a part to play in their more formal lessons concerned with language and number. As well as helping the young children to explore basic groups and sets, teddy bears were finding a role in developing measuring and weighing skills among the older children. Creative writing about teddy bears was being assembled on display boards to arrange round the church.

Nearer the day, the chancel of the church was taken over to make a picnic area. A carpet of artificial grass (borrowed from a friendly undertaker) was placed on the floor. Picnic benches and tables were made from cardboard boxes. Real moss and flowers were collected and arranged. Small logs and branches were strewed around. A notice was made proclaiming 'picnic area'.

On the Friday before the picnic, much of the school day was given over to baking and to preparing food. In particular, a large supply of biscuits was baked in teddy bear shapes.

Parents had been given plenty of notice by the school that the project was going to reach its climax in church on Sunday in the Parish Communion. When the Sunday arrived, lots more children and lots more teddy bears came to the service than usual.

The service opened with the hymn 'Morning has broken' and the introductory part of the communion service was conducted as usual up to, but not including, the collect. At this point the teddy bears were invited to come to the picnic area in the chancel and to take their places among the picnic tables and benches. The children from the school also brought to the picnic area small table cloths and some of the food they had prepared.

After the picnic area had been thoroughly prepared, the children from the top class presented their drama and dance, dressed in their teddy bear costumes. Their dance reached its climax when one of the children brought in a huge yellow sun on a tall pole and held it high in the middle of the picnic scene. The whole congregation then sang 'The Teddy Bears' Picnic' to a musical background of percussion, chime bars and recorders.

The teddy bears' enjoyment of their picnic enabled the adults and children in the congregation to explore some of the power of the image of feasting in the Christian tradition, especially as this relates to the Messianic banquet and to the eucharist itself. This part of the service culminated in the reading of the story of the feeding of the five thousand from St John's gospel and the singing of the eucharistic hymn 'Alleluia sing to Jesus'.

After this hymn the teddy bears were left picnicking in the chancel and the focus of attention in the service was changed. A table was placed in front of the chancel screen to act as a nave altar. Once again children came forward with a table cloth, but this time to cover the altar. Once again children came forward with food, but this time carrying the bread and the wine of the eucharist. When the children had prepared the table for the celebration of communion, the formal liturgy resumed with the eucharistic prayer.

After the distribution of communion and after the post communion prayers, but before the final hymn, the nave altar was removed and the picnicking teddy bears again became the focus of attention. Some of the children returned to the musical instruments and again began to play teddy bear music. Others came into the picnic area and collected baskets containing the bear-shaped biscuits. They distributed these biscuits to the adults and children throughout the congregation, so that the whole worshipping community could share in the feasting of the teddy bears' picnic.

For the final hymn, 'All creatures of our God and King', the children were invited to reclaim their teddy bears and to hold them aloft. Those who had not brought a teddy bear with them or who did not want to hold their teddy bear were invited to have a percussion instrument to provide a background rhythm for the hymn.

The children went home with the dismissal and blessing ringing in their ears:

the blessing of God almighty,
the Father, the Son and the Holy Spirit,
be among you,
and remain with you and your teddy bears always.

As far as the children of the school were concerned, the teddy bears' picnic had been an enjoyable project. Over a period of time it had involved almost all the components of their varied curriculum, from numbers to language, from drama to dance, from music to craft, from painting to knitting, from cooking to woodwork. As far as the local church was concerned, the teddy bears' picnic had given the children an opportunity to make full use of the church building and to participate in formal liturgy adapted to their own level. The occasion had, in fact, brought many children into contact with the Parish Communion who had never previously been to a communion service. At the same time, the specific theme of the picnic had provided an ideal opportunity to lay some of the essential foundations of eucharistic teaching.

Consequence

Not only did I invite the children of the school and parish to bring their teddy bears to the teddy bears' picnic, I took my own teddy bear along as well. My teddy bear so enjoyed the occasion that he began to pester me to find other opportunities for him to join in the worship of my church. Then he managed to recruit a teddy bear from my godson's family into the conspiracy, a teddy bear known as Teddy Horsley.

Before long Teddy Horsley was looking for opportunities to explore the rich imagery and language of the church's worship. He thought through his adventure at the teddy bears' picnic and began to think theologically about the close parallels between his experiences at the picnic and his experiences at the eucharist. Soon Teddy Horsley was asking whether Nicola Slee and I could help him write down his thoughts. And so the Teddy Horsley series was born.

When Teddy Horsley goes picnicking with his family, Lucy, Walter, Mr and Mrs Henry and Betsy Bear, they take bread to eat and lemonade and wine to drink. They munch, they chatter, they laugh: they celebrate their picnic. Everyone is happy. When Teddy Horsley goes to church with his family, they bring bread on a silver plate, wine in a silver cup to the altar. They sing, they worship, they share: they celebrate the communion. Everyone is happy. Mr and Mrs Henry lead some prayers, Lucy and Walter play their instruments, while Teddy Horsley and Betsy Bear play under the pew.

By taking the concrete image of the picnic, Teddy Horsley is able to grasp one of the central ideas of the communion service. By building on children's concrete experiences of picnics, Teddy Horsley is able to help them make the transition from everyday secular experience to religious experience. In other words, he is developing their religious vocabulary from the everyday secular language which lies at the heart of our interpretation of religious experience.

The next religious idea in which Teddy Horsley took an interest was the concept of the Holy Spirit at Pentecost. Just as he built up his idea of communion from the concrete experience of going to a picnic, so he looked around for the concrete everyday experience which lies at the heart of the Christian language about God the Holy Spirit. This time Teddy Horsley focused on the image of the wind.

Images of the wind have historically played a very central part in the development of the church's theology of God the Holy Spirit; the link between the secular experience of the wind and the religious experience of the Spirit of God is in fact so close that in both the Hebrew and the Greek languages the same word is used for wind and for Spirit. In Hebrew the one word used to speak of both the wind and the Spirit is *ruach*; in Greek the one word is *pneuma*.

Without knowing anything about Greek or Hebrew, Teddy Horsley recognised the essential qualities which God the Holy Spirit and the wind have in common. On a windy day Teddy Horsley opens his eyes to look for the wind, but he cannot see it. But he sees the wind shake apples down, turn washing inside out and blow paper along the street. He stretches out his paws to touch the wind and cannot feel it. But he feels the wind push him along, tug his kite into the sky and drive rain into his face. He pricks up his ears to listen to the wind and cannot hear it, but he hears the wind rattle dustbin lids, slam doors shut and whistle through trees. Although he can neither see, touch nor hear the wind, Teddy Horsley knows that the wind is there, all around him.

Similarly, Teddy Horsley discovers that he can neither see, touch nor hear God the Holy Spirit. But he does see the Holy Spirit making people smile and dance. He does feel the Holy Spirit making him safe and loved. He does hear the Holy Spirit making people sing and laugh. Through these signs of the Holy Spirit's activity in the world, Teddy Horsley comes to know that the Holy Spirit is there, all around him, just like the wind.

After exploring the great Christian festival of Pentecost, Teddy Horsley became restless to explore the other central feasts of the

Christian year. He begins with Easter and then goes on to explore Christmas.

At the heart of the gospel message of Easter, Teddy Horsley finds the simple basic concept of new life. One sunny morning, Teddy Horsley wakes up and comes down to the breakfast table, feeling full of life. He skips into the open fields with Lucy, Walter and Betsy Bear. Once out into the countryside he sees all the signs of new life. He gambols with the new born lambs in the fields. He watches the birds building their nests in the trees. He plays with the young rabbits on the path. He talks with the sleepy hedgehog and tortoise emerging from hibernation. He stretches up tall to see the new leaves on the trees and bends down low to touch the budding wild flowers. All around him, Teddy Horsley sees the new signs of life. Teddy Horsley himself shares in the new life of the morning.

On Easter Sunday Teddy Horsley again comes down to the breakfast table, feeling full of life. He skips to church with Lucy, Walter and Betsy Bear. In church he sees the Easter garden, with all the colourful spring flowers. He sees the big empty tomb in the Easter garden and runs into it to touch the folded grave clothes. He stretches up tall to see the flame of the Paschal candle and bends down low to touch the water running through the garden. He hears the good news of the resurrection. All around him in the Easter garden Teddy Horsley sees the signs of new life. Teddy Horsley himself shares in the new life of Easter.

At the heart of the gospel message of Christmas, Teddy Horsley finds the simple and basic concept of light, following the lead of St John in the prologue to the fourth gospel. Before Christmas, during early December, Teddy Horsley runs into town to see the lights of Christmas with Mr and Mrs Henry, Lucy, Walter and Betsy Bear. He gazes at the lights flashing in shop windows and laughs at the banners sparkling in the streets. He warms his paws by the fire in the market place and dances to the colourful lights in the square. He is dazzled by the bright floodlights on the town hall and welcomed by the soft lamps in the cafe. He points up to the star gleaming high on the tree in the town centre and kneels down low to see the coloured lights streaming through the branches. Teddy Horsley is glad to see the lights of Christmas.

Then Teddy Horsley goes into church with Mr and Mrs Henry, Lucy, Walter and Betsy Bear. Inside he finds a huge Christmas crib scene. Against the large colourful collage backcloth depicting Bethlehem and the surrounding countryside, he sees life-like crib figures made from paper sculpture, as large as he is. He goes up to the shepherds who are watching over the sheep in the green pasture and warms his paws by their fire. He dances to the light of the shepherds' lanterns. He is dazzled by the bright angels in the sky and welcomed by the soft lamps of the Bethlehem inn. He points up at the star gleaming over the stable. He kneels down low to see the light streaming from the manger and worships the Christ child in the crib. Teddy Horsley is glad to see the Light of Christmas.

Conclusion

By developing the relationship between concrete everyday experiences and the theological and liturgical concepts of the church, Teddy Horsley has been gradually expanding the Christian vocabulary and understanding of the young people in the church congregation and in the church school.

Teddy bears like being with real children, and I would not be all that surprised if right now Teddy Horsley and his friends were experimenting and exploring other concrete everyday experiences of the nursery and discovering that they too hold the key to further theological and liturgical concepts. Looking back, I am very grateful to Susan's teddy bear for so roughly drawing my attention to his presence in the parish communion. I am only sorry that I had overlooked him for so long and failed to appreciate his considerable potential contribution to the Christian nurture of the young.

10 CHURCH PRIMARY SCHOOLS

Leslie J. Francis

Context

Our village school was founded by the rector of the parish long before the 1870 Education Act set up local board schools. The trust deed of the school clearly reflected the foundation aims of the National Society, namely to establish schools "for the education of the poor in the principles of the established church".

When the 1944 Education Act reaffirmed the partnership between the churches and the state in the provision of a state maintained system of schools, the managers of our village schools opted for voluntary aided status. This meant that the church was still able to appoint a *majority* of the managers, that the daily act of worship in school assembly could be clearly denominational and that denominational religious instruction could be given throughout the school to all pupils, except in those cases where parents specifically requested that alternative provision should be made. The other part of the voluntary aided bargain meant that the church was still responsible for finding half of the money needed to maintain, or where necessary extend, the school building.

In the early 1960s the recommended repairs and modifications to the school building were regarded as beyond the financial commitment which the managers were able or willing to consider. As a consequence, the managers decided to relinquish voluntary aided status and accept voluntary controlled status. This meant that the church was still able to appoint a *minority* of the managers and maintain a daily act of denominational worship. Denominational religious instruction was now replaced by religious instruction according to the local education authority's agreed syllabus, except for those children whose parents specifically requested withdrawal classes for denominational lessons.

Against this background, the rector had remained chairman of the managers, conducted an assembly each week and continued to take the top class of seven to eleven year olds for a weekly period of religious instruction. When I arrived in the parish as priest-in-charge the headteacher asked me, I think with a little trepidation, whether I wished to continue with the weekly assembly and the weekly period of religious instruction. I declined the invitation, but asked to be able to talk with the headteacher and with the one other full-time member of staff in this two teacher school about possibilities of working together 'after I had begun to settle in'.

Possibilities

Church controlled schools can still be a great blessing for the local church, but they cannot be regarded as an automatic annexe to the local church's work. Church controlled schools are today first and foremost part of the national network of secular educational provision. Teachers in church controlled schools are first and foremost part of the autonomous teaching profession.

Although our village school had been founded by the local parish church, I had to acknowledge that the majority of the pupils attending that school today had no natural links with the parent church which had founded the school. Some pupils were bussed in from neighbouring parishes and possibly related to the worshipping life of another medieval parish church and possibly came under the active care of another Anglican priest. Some pupils lived in the neighbouring hamlet where the Brethren chapel had been long established and some of them, I knew, attended the Brethren Sunday school. Some of the pupils living in the centre of the village were within the network of the small Methodist Sunday school. Many of the thirty-five pupils did not relate regularly to any form of church, nor did their parents.

A church controlled school cannot, therefore, assume the Christian background of its pupils, nor the goodwill of parents that a Christian ethos should dominate the school itself. After all, parents send their children to this school, first and foremost, not because it is a *church* school but because it is the *only* school serving the neighbourhood.

The professional status of teaching has also changed radically since our village school was founded by the rector in the 1850s. One of the consequences of this is that it is less easy for the rector to go into the local church school for one hour a week and to do a professional educational job which holds credibility alongside the full-time teachers. My own approach has not been to intrude into the school for an hour a week, but to discover what the school itself is doing and to explore how, together with the full-time staff, the local church can help develop this on-going programme.

My first term in the parish was the autumn term, leading up to Christmas. The school was already well used to the idea of preparing a Christmas event to share with parents at the end of term. This generally took place in the village hall on a weekday afternoon, or on a weekday evening to allow more parents to attend. This year, the Christmas event had been stimulated by the school's radio project on the old Russian tradition of Baboushka. My suggestion was simply that the end of term project should be held in church on a Sunday evening, at 6 o'clock in place of Evensong. The school took it from there.

The initiative for the project was to be with the school staff themselves; my job was to listen to their enthusiasm, encourage them to feel free to use the church building to the full and to make certain gentle suggestions. The important thing was for the church not to take over the initiative, but to respect the fact that the teachers were the professional educationalists in the community. On the last Sunday of term the pupils from the school, their parents and the local church congregation assembled together to celebrate their preparation for Christmas in a rather different way from previous years. The celebration included some traditional carols, but it also included the story, mime, drama, dance and music stimulated by the school's radio programme.

This Sunday evening before Christmas demonstrated that church and school could work together and that they could do so on terms that were totally acceptable to both sides. The children of the school were being gently introduced to the life of their parish church; the parents did not feel that they were being cajoled into church attendance. Parents who wanted to treat the Baboushka evening as an act of worship could do so; those who preferred to see it as an end of term school concert were equally able to do so. But as far as the local church was concerned, the event had a considerable spin-off for the rest of the Christmas services.

Palm Sunday

Because the first joint church and school project had been enjoyable and because the local church had been careful not to take too much for granted, it was comparatively easy to begin planning a joint venture for the end of the next term, just before Easter.

This term the school was working on a project about the Romans, to coincide with an educational programme mounted by the local museum. This meant that there was already in the school a substantial backcloth of work on life in the Roman empire. The events of Holy Week and Easter, in the Roman occupied Jerusalem, seemed to fit in ideally against this backcloth. School term was not going to finish until Holy Week, so we decided to work together towards a joint school-church project for Palm Sunday.

The pupils were reminded of the stories of Palm Sunday and Holy Week and they began to think how they could interpret these traditions and present them to their parents and the local church congregation. The presentation which emerged was based on creating 'media coverage' of the event.

A small group of the older pupils emerged as 'reporters from the Holy Mail'. Their idea was that they would follow Jesus through the events of Palm Sunday and Holy Week, but always arriving on the scene just after Jesus had moved on. This would give them the opportunity to interview the people who had been with Jesus or who had witnessed his actions or heard his words, but they would never actually catch up with Jesus himself.

The rest of the pupils formed the groups whom the reporters would meet and with whom they would talk. By the time I came on the scene, the pupils had worked out eight short scenarios:

1 they interview the owner of the donkey on which Christ rode into Jerusalem;
2 they visit the home of Martha and Mary in Bethany, the

village in which Jesus is said to have stayed during Holy Week;

3   they talk with the money-changers and stall-holders around the temple;

4   they talk with the servants and householders of the place where Jesus celebrated the Passover;

5   they intercept some of the disciples fleeing from Gethsemane after the arrest;

6   they follow the soldiers into the trial and talk with the disciple who denies that he knows Jesus;

7   outside they talk with the Roman guards;

8   they arrive at Calvary after the crucifixion and meet with the soldiers who have taken possession of Jesus' clothes.

These scenes included a basic script, actions and music. Sometimes the answers to the reporters' questions came in song rather than in narrative.

When all this had been prepared, I needed to liaise with the teachers to discover how we could employ the pupils' initiatives within a celebration in which both their parents and the church congregation could join.

We decided to begin the Palm Sunday celebration by inviting parents and congregation to assemble in the school playground by 6.00 p.m. The school playground was alive with small Roman soldiers, parading the banners of their legion. At 6 o'clock precisely, a pupil trumpeter signalled a fanfare. The hymn 'All glory, laud and honour' was played through and the procession moved off towards the church singing. There in the procession was the donkey who lived at the Old Rectory.

The celebration, therefore, began with a great deal of excitement. Our first strategic problem was to channel this excitement and settle children and adults down in the church once they had arrived. We thought it important that the entry into church set the right tone for the rest of the evening. As we stepped into church, our attention was caught both by sound and vision. A local doctor (complete with his telephone bleep system, because he was on duty) was playing meditative 'Roman' music on his guitar. The leader of the neighbouring Brethren Sunday school was projecting a sequence of colour slides of Jerusalem onto the large screen which filled the chancel arch, for now the parish church had become Roman occupied Jerusalem. As soon as we were all in church we concluded our Palm Sunday procession by singing 'Ride on! ride on in majesty!'.

While the pupils of the school had plenty of opportunity to participate in the celebration, through their preparation at school and through the scenes they had developed, I was conscious that there was a danger that the church congregation and parents might feel like spectators rather than participants. We decided, therefore, to script the whole congregation into the celebration as the chorus, which could provide the continuity between the eight separate scenarios developed by the pupils.

Since there is a danger that unrehearsed choral speech will not stay rhythmically together for very long, the chorus was designed as a series of short versicles and responses, between one leader and the whole of the congregation. Together the leader and the congregation identified themselves with the crowd.

The first chorus, therefore, establishes the congregation's identity as part of the pilgrim people coming into Jerusalem:

> We have come as pilgrims,
> *pilgrims to Jerusalem.*
> We have come to the end of our journey,
> *the journey from our homes and villages.*
> We have followed a borrowed donkey,
> *a borrowed donkey and a dusty rider.*
> We have travelled along the winding road,
> *over the running brook,*
> through the city gate,
> *inside the city wall.*
> We have waved our branches of palm
> *and scattered our coats in the road.*
> We have shouted Hosanna,
> *Hosanna to the King of Kings.*

As the 'Hosanna to the King of Kings' dies away so the reporters come to the centre and plan how they are going to cover the Jesus story. One of them goes immediately to the south porch of the church to talk with the owner of the donkey on which they had heard that Jesus had ridden into Jerusalem. Alas, the reporters arrive too late to witness the procession in which the whole of the church had taken part!

The second chorus moves the scene from Jerusalem to the village where Jesus is staying overnight. The crowd looks in on their supper time:

> The day light is faded
> *and evening is here.*
> Come, gather outside the house,
> *the house where Mary and Martha live.*
> Come, stand by the window,
> *peep through the lattice.*
> Inside the lamps are lit;
> *the table is set.*
> We will watch the guests enjoy their supper;
> *we will listen to their conversation.*
> We will watch their festivity
> *and join in their singing.*

This chorus leads into Sidney Carter's song 'Judas and Mary'. Then the reporters interview Mary and go into the kitchen to find Martha. Mary and Martha speak about Jesus as part of their lives and the congregation pick up their comments about Jesus' gentle friendship by singing the hymn 'Jesus, good above all other'.

The third chorus takes the scene back to Jerusalem, this time to the temple:

> Here we will stand close by the temple,
> *the temple where the pilgrims meet,*
> the temple where the money changers give short change,
> *the temple where birds are sold for sacrifice,*
> the temple where the Passover lamb is killed,
> *the temple where thanksgiving is offered to God,*
> the temple where Jesus teaches the people,
> *the temple where Jesus upsets the leaders.*
> Here we will listen to the uproar
> *and watch the commotion.*

Outside the reporters chat with a cobbler selling sandals, with the money-changers and with those selling birds for sacrifice. They hear about the way Jesus upset their stalls and drove them from the temple.

The fourth chorus takes us on to the Maundy Thursday passover meal:

Time moves on. We have roasted the passover lamb
and the passover meal has been eaten.
We have eaten the lamb
and remembered our forefathers' escape from Egypt.
We have eaten bitter herbs
and remembered our forefathers' suffering.
We have eaten unleavened bread
and remembered our forefathers' haste.
Jesus, too, has celebrated Passover with his disciples
and shared broken bread with his friends.
But now the party is over
and the servants are preparing for another day.

Again the reporters arrive too late, but they are able to talk with the servants and with the householders who are sharing the job of clearing up after the supper. Fortunately, there are plenty of Matzo meal biscuits left over from the supper; the servants share these biscuits with the reporters and then with the whole congregation. In this way we all have the opportunity to take part in the supper.

The fifth chorus conveys us with the disciples to Gethsemane:

Again we have arrived too late;
Jesus has left the party.
Come, let us follow him to Gethsemane,
to Gethsemane on the Mount of Olives.
Here let us slip into the shadows
to watch among the olive trees.
Here let us keep awake,
awake to watch.
Here let us keep awake,
awake to pray.

By the time the reporters arrive on the scene in Gethsemane, they learn that Jesus has already been arrested. They intercept a disciple or two as they scatter in confusion through the dark garden.

The sixth chorus has us shivering in the night air and attempting to warm ourselves by the fire in the courtyard while Jesus' trial goes on:

> The night is growing darker;
> *the air is growing colder.*
> The soldiers have led away their prisoner;
> *the disciples have fled to safety.*
> We, too, will follow the crowd;
> *we will follow the noise;*
> We will follow the commotion;
> *we will follow the jeering;*
> We will follow into the courtyard
> *and warm ourselves by the fire.*

Now the reporters from the Holy Mail find Peter. They identify his accent, but all they learn from Peter is the strong denial that he has anything to do with Jesus. Then they talk with the Roman soldiers who dismiss Jesus as a trouble maker, a 'nutter'. As the trial goes on, the congregation sings 'There is a green hill far away'.

Then the last chorus is our invitation to travel those final steps of the journey to Calvary itself:

> Here we will stand close by Calvary,
> *Calvary where they plant the crosses in the ground,*
> Calvary where they crucify Jesus,
> *Calvary where they crucify the two robbers,*
> Calvary where the soldiers share out their spoil,
> *Calvary where the soldiers throw dice,*
> Calvary where the sun grows dark,
> *Calvary where life stops.*
>
> O, Saviour of the world,
> by your cross and passion you have redeemed us.
> *Save us and help us, we pray you, Lord.*

After interviewing the soldiers who took part in the crucifixion and who shared out Jesus' clothes among themselves, the reporters reassemble to try to piece together their story. They are tired; they are somewhat confused. The man whose life they had been following is now dead. Some of them are uneasy that they have not yet heard the end of the matter. Now the congregation comes in with Sidney Carter's hymn 'Lord of the dance'; and the joint church-school celebration has reached its climax.

Conclusion

A celebration of this nature meant a great deal of careful preparation and close co-operation between church and school. Neither side had a clear idea what would emerge, but both had a firm commitment to ensuring that the end product was worthy both of high professional educational standards and of the local church foregoing its customary liturgy on such a major festival as Palm Sunday. In a very real sense our Palm Sunday procession was a journey of faith.

11 SECULAR SECONDARY SCHOOLS

Leslie J. Francis

Limitations

During the 1970s and the 1980s considerable changes in educational theory and practice have accentuated the gap between the churches and the secular school. There are three key ways in which this gap has been widened. First, strong arguments have been advanced to support the case that school worship is an inappropriate activity within a religiously pluralist and predominantly secular culture; today recognisably Christian worship is less and less likely to take place in the school assembly. Second, the aims and objectives of religious education have been redefined in order to replace the confessional aim of religious education assumed to be appropriate at the time of the 1944 Education Act with educational aims deemed appropriate within the secular school; today religious education aims to teach *about* world religions not to make pupils religious in any one specific tradition. Third, the emergence of educational theory as an autonomous discipline in its own right has emphasised the case that theological principles should not be allowed to influence educational decisions; today what counts as good educational practice or as appropriate curriculum content needs to be determined wholly on educational criteria, not on religious criteria.

Whether these three arguments should be regarded as right or wrong is not the essential issue at stake. The plain fact of the matter is that these arguments are increasingly carrying weight in determining what is happening in the secular secondary school. Of course, there are secular schools in which Christian teachers are making a wide range of Christian contributions to the educational, personal and social development of the pupils. But it would be very unwise for the churches to lose sight of the fact that they can no longer assume a Christian presence in the secular secondary school as a matter of right. The churches cannot assume that school assemblies are providing opportunities for Christian worship, that religious education lessons are presenting the challenge of the Christian faith or that the hidden curriculum and the pervading school ethos are communicating Christian values.

One of the main responses of the churches to this situation has been to develop the distinction between the concepts of 'education' and 'nurture'. It is often now argued that secular schools should be left to get on with their professional job of education, while the churches and parents should be left to get on with their job of nurture. This distinction might have two important implications. First, the church would have very little formal contact with young people during the school day while they are attending the secular secondary school. Second, the church would attempt to organise a range of catechetical and church-based recreational activities outside the school day, presumably conducted on church premises and resourced by professional and lay church personnel.

In some senses this is a sensible distinction and a very realistic response on the part of the churches. In other senses, however, I find this argument less than satisfactory, and that for two reasons. First, I have found that the churches with which I have worked have lacked the resources necessary to organise adequate opportunities for young people outside the school day. While the theory that the churches should attend to their own Christian nurture programme sounds good, the implementation of this theory is too often thwarted both by the churches' inability to provide the environment and the professional leadership and by the busy teenagers' inability or unwillingness to take part in such programmes. Second, I am reluctant to accept the notion that there cannot be opportunities for the church and school to meet upon terms that are both educationally acceptable to the secular school and religiously acceptable to the worshipping community.

I have wanted to explore, therefore, ways in which it might still be possible for the church to work in some co-operation with the local secular secondary school. Since the church cannot assume a right to work with the secular secondary school, it is important that initiatives taken by the church should thoroughly respect the educational autonomy of the school and not attempt to work against the educational theory or professional practice which the school represents. In practice this means two things. Whatever initiative the church takes can only be implemented with the complete goodwill, trust and confidence of the headteacher and staff. If these relationships are wrong, there are few possibilities for access and none for success. Second, the church must accept the restriction not to attempt to proselytise or evangelise among non-church members through the secular school.

However, even given these fairly severe restrictions on what the church might like to be able to do, a great deal can still be accomplished. In order to realise these possibilities, it is necessary to draw a clear distinction between what the church can do when given the opportunity to work in schools specifically among church members and what it can legitimately do when it is given the opportunity to work in schools among mixed groups of pupils, including church members and non-church members. I propose to examine these two areas of possibility in turn.

Christian groups

In many secular schools the lunch break and the time immediately at the end of the school day provide opportunities for extra curricula activities. At these points in the school day a range of sporting, social, recreational and educational activities take place. Some groups are intentionally set up by members of staff; others are wholly sponsored by the pupils themselves. Pupils come to these groups because they want to do so. While they are held on school premises, they stand, in a sense, outside the closer scrutiny of educational theory and practice.

Within the context of such voluntary activities the school Christian Union has had a long and helpful tradition. School Christian Unions vary greatly in their theological and social emphases and may sometimes appear to be at variance with the perspectives of the local Anglican churches. However, even when the Christian Union adopts a theological position with which the local church may feel uncomfortable, it seems to me exceedingly careless and short-sighted of the local church not to show as much interest in the group as possible. After all, the Christian

Union may be the only public face of the Christian churches visible to the pupils within the school itself.

In the last analysis, school Christian Unions take on their character from the pupils who support them and from the members of the school staff who resource them. At one stage, I had the good fortune of realising that the member of staff responsible for the Christian Union in the local secondary school lived in one of my parishes and played an important part in the life of my church. Although our theological positions were rather different, we found that we could work together. This gave me the opportunity to go in to the occasional Christian Union meeting. It also gave me the opportunity to invite the Christian Union to contribute to the worship of my church on several occasions. Since this meant recruiting young people from other parishes and from the congregations of other denominations, this was not a practice which it was wise to repeat too often. Yet, on the right occasions, it offered the young people a taste of worship which differed from their usual pattern and also offered my congregation an opportunity to worship alongside more young people than they were accustomed to meet in their village church.

In addition to the Christian Union there are also a range of other contexts in which young Christians may be able to come together during the lunch break or at the end of the day in the secular school. For example, in one secular secondary school in which I was doing a short spell of supply teaching, while the religious education specialist was in hospital, I was taken by surprise on my first day at the end of the morning session. A group of six or seven pupils came to my classroom and told me that they were accustomed to meet every day at this time with the religious education teacher to say the Angelus. I joined them, and looked forward to their return the next day.

In another school in which I worked on supply teaching from time to time, I discovered that the religious education teacher, who was also a non-stipendiary Anglican priest, had developed the pattern of a lunch time eucharist just once a month in a classroom. This informal eucharist had helped to create a real sense of identity among a group of churchgoing pupils recruited from a large number of different churches. On the other hand, when I tried to transfer this practice to a similar secondary school the headteacher refused me permission to do so. This headteacher was in fact churchwarden of an Anglican church; his objection was not to the Christian practice, but to allowing any religious or political organisation to arrange activities in his school. His argument was that, if he allowed the Anglican priest to celebrate eucharist at lunch time in school, he would also have to allow other religious and political groups to hold their own sectarian meetings. He envisaged that if he allowed me to have a classroom at lunch time, he would also have to allow the leaders of the local Jehovah Witnesses and of the local Conservative party. No amount of argument would change his view. What the local church is allowed to do in a secular secondary school, even among its own adherents, is strictly dependent upon the views and goodwill of the headteacher and the school staff.

For Christian groups to flourish in the secular secondary school, they need ideally to be organised by a member of staff within the school itself. Local clergy and members of the local congregation can then be invited to resource the group in specific ways, but the group itself is always seen as something indigenous to the school rather than being imposed in some sense from outside. Given the willingness of Christian members of staff to work alongside the local churches in this kind of way, all sorts of exciting possibilities can follow. The possibility of belonging to such a group may be particularly important for the teenage churchgoer who worships on a Sunday in a small congregation, say in a village, and who has little opportunity to identify with other committed teenagers in his or her own church.

In a slightly more general sense, once young people move away from their immediate neighbourhood to attend a secondary school, the school itself tends to become the unit which defines their social point of reference, rather than where they live. It is the school which determines much of their friendship patterns. There is a lot to be said in favour of the church recognising the implication of these groupings when thinking in terms, for example, of arranging confirmation preparation or church-based teenage social activities. If neighbouring parishes could find ways of agreeing on a common strategy in this sense, their pastoral effectiveness among young people could be increased.

Mixed groups

The ways in which it is appropriate for the local churches to work in the secular secondary school with mixed groups, including both churchgoers and non-churchgoers, are quite different from the ways appropriate with voluntary groups of committed pupils. In this context, the church must work in line with the educational criteria established by the school. In practice this often means not assuming the willingness of pupils to engage in Christian worship, nor assuming the right to teach religious doctrines as incontrovertible truths. Honouring these restrictions, there is still a range of ways in which I have found it possible to foster links between the secular secondary school and the local church.

One of the most obvious ways to build relationships between school and church is by developing the church building itself as a central local resource. For example, the history department in the school may welcome the opportunity to develop project work on the history of the local church, concentrating on styles of architecture, parish records, the life-styles of previous vicars and their congregations. The art department may welcome the opportunity to study the vestments, the silver and the stained glass, as well as encouraging the pupils to sketch or paint aspects of the interior or exterior of the church. Similar opportunities may be welcomed by school groups concerned with photography. While the religious education department itself may strongly refuse to share the church's task of teaching the Christian faith, it is likely to welcome the opportunity to demonstrate to the pupils what Christian buildings and Christian worship are like. The local church can play a key part in the 'objective' study of the Christian tradition.

In less obvious ways, the English department may value the opportunity to use the church building to practise reading or choral speech under different acoustic conditions. The maths department may find the church tower an ideal landmark on which to practise the calculation of height in basic trigonometry. Environmental studies may take an interest in the churchyard, while social studies might consider arranging tape recorded interviews with members of a Parochial Church Council, regarding their perceptions of the rôle of the church in the local community, or with senior members of the congregation, regarding their recollections of changes in the worship and life of their local church. The music department might find occasions when it would benefit from using the church organ.

A local church can do a great deal to promote this sort of use of the church building by developing the right kind of personal relationships with the appropriate members of the school staff and by working alongside the staff to produce the right kind of learning material. For example, school and church might jointly develop a project-based programme to explore the local church building. While the development of such resource material is time consuming, well produced material can provide the basis for work with different groups over several years.

A second obvious resource is the clergyman himself. What the clergyman is able to do in the school naturally depends on both the peculiar skills of the individual clergyman and the peculiar needs of individual schools. Not all clergymen are skilled and trained in secondary education. In many senses this is a pastoral area which needs to be regarded as a specialist ministry. Since many secular secondary schools draw pupils from across a number of parish boundaries, it might well be sensible for the clergy involved to appoint one of their number, who has the appropriate professional training, to act as a kind of informal chaplain to the local school.

Being a qualified teacher, I have been able to make myself available to local schools as a supply teacher. Sometimes I have deputised for the religious education staff, but more usually for a secular subject, like English or maths or once even for needlework. In this way I have met pupils from non-church backgrounds on their own territory and on their own terms. My presence in the classroom has not been an intrusion. I have been there with a specific task to fulfil like all the other teachers. At the same time, the clerical collar has been the symbol to open up specific discussions with groups or with individuals.

On other occasions I have been deliberately invited into the school, for example by the sixth form general studies department to contribute to discussion or projects on a range of issues regarding which the church might be thought to have a distinctive contribution to make. These have not been occasions to lecture, but opportunities to listen to debate and to make a specific contribution as and when the pupils appear to welcome it.

The most valuable resource of all, however, is not what the church can bring into the school from outside, but the on-going life of the school itself which can, from time to time, be focused on the local church. Schools are so often full of resourceful and creative people. The church needs to be in touch with the points of vibrant creativity within the school and gently explore whether the school is willing to allow the local church to benefit from this. A range of specific occasions come to mind when schools have willingly resourced my own churches.

When I first assumed responsibility for one small village church, I inherited a small congregation struggling to sing its hymns. In order to give a lift to liturgy on my first Easter Sunday in that church, I asked a teacher from the local secular secondary school if he could recruit a group of singers to come to my church just on that one occasion. He recruited eight or nine pupils from the sixth form, none from within my own parish and most of them not committed to a church of any sort. They transformed the hymn singing in the service, contributed their own unaccompanied anthem during the communion of the people, and then stayed on for lunch afterwards.

For the next festival, instead of recruiting a choir from the school, I explored the possibility of recruiting a small string orchestra to provide music before and after the service and during the communion of the people. Again a group of pupils came together from a variety of backgrounds to offer this specific contribution to my church. Later in the year, the church invited the musicians back to mount an evening concert. On this occasion we arranged an interval which was long enough for musicians and congregation to share refreshments together.

In a completely different context I had the opportunity to work with the music specialist of a local middle school, catering for the third and fourth year junior and first and second year secondary age range. The school was interested in learning and performing Michael Hurd's 'Jonah-man Jazz'. We decided to arrange an evening performance in church when the school would be almost totally responsible for the organisation. In some senses, the church was being used by the school as their concert hall. I encouraged them to use the organ in their performance and to display related art and craft material to transform the church into an appropriate sea-scape. A huge net was draped over the rood-screen and filled with silver fish.

The decorations were kept in the church for the following Sunday and the Jonah tradition was adopted for the theme for the Parish Communion. I invited the pupils to come back to that Sunday service and to present parts of the Jonah-man Jazz in the context of the Parish Communion. The complete choir and orchestra did not turn up on the Sunday morning, but a sufficient proportion of them did to make the venture more than worthwhile.

In a similar way, one year I discovered that the drama department of a local secular secondary school was preparing a set of material on the secular and sacred interpretation of Christmas, involving components of poetry, song, mime, dance, drama, humour and even worship. Again the school was willing for the church to take an interest in what was being created and offered to come to repeat their Christmas presentation in the church itself.

The observant visitor to the well organised school is often impressed by the range of the pupils' work displayed in the foyer, in the hall, classrooms or sixth form common-room. In visiting local schools, I became aware of the potential of asking schools if they would be willing to lend some of their display material to the church. A particularly good time to do this is just before the Christmas or Easter holiday. Particularly at Christmas time the school is likely to have produced some display material which is relevant to the church's liturgical year, and the school often wishes to dismantle this material before the holiday begins.

One Christmas I discovered that the local middle school had transformed the school hall into a nativity scene. A wall was covered with a huge mural composed of combined painting and collage effects, showing Bethlehem and the neighbouring hillside. The mural acted as a backcloth for some superb figures made from paper sculpture. Kings and shepherds and angels had been sculptured in child-sized proportions. The school was wondering what to do with these figures at the very time I tentatively asked if the church could borrow them for its Christmas services.

Bringing these huge crib figures into church helped the pupils of the middle school to feel that the local church was interested in what they were doing and I suspect actively encouraged some of the pupils to bring their parents along to the church's carol service!

Conclusion

In an age when the church finds it increasingly difficult to maintain contact with teenagers, the secular secondary school should perhaps be seen as a vital link in the local church's overall pastoral strategy. There are, of course, no guarantees that the church will be made welcome. On the other hand, the chances of a welcome are considerably higher if the local church first takes the trouble both to become familiar with the educational theory and principles on which the secular secondary school operates and to demonstrate its own integrity in personal relationships with the headteacher and staff long before it attempts to work with the pupils. Today the secular educational system may well still be open to co-operation with the church, but not to exploitation by the church.

12 DANCE

Nicola Slee

Context

My interest in liturgical dance began in my early teens. A series of
dance workshops at a young people's summer camp opened the
door to a whole new world, as I discovered that my body need
not be an irrelevance or encumbrance in worship, but is the God-
given vehicle of self-discovery, self-expression and self-offering.

As a student the chance to develop this interest further came
through a small liturgical dance group which met weekly. We
were a small group, never more than six; although mostly
students, there were also a vet and a housewife and mother; all
but one of us were female. Most of us had no formal dance
background. We shared the fruits of our weekly meeting with the
congregation of a city church, dancing in the Sunday eucharist
once a term. Gradually other opportunities evolved. We were
asked to conduct workshops in parishes and colleges, with adults
and teenagers.

In this chapter I shall describe one of our typical workshops
arranged primarily for teenagers. On this occasion we had been
invited to the parish of St Andrew on the outskirts of Cambridge to share a day's programme for Pathfinders and their
leaders on the use of the arts in Christian development. About
one hundred people were expected: seventy-five teenagers and
their leaders. They would be given the chance to explore the
use of dance, drama, music, choral reading, creative writing, crafts, painting and much more. At the end of the day a
special service of celebration was planned for the whole gathering, at which different groups would offer some of the day's
work.

Aims

As we prepared for our day at St Andrew's church, an important distinction emerged between two main aims or functions of the dance workshop; and eventually we decided to hold two separate workshops, one for each aim.

The first aim of the dance workshop is to enable teenagers and adults to explore and develop the use of dance for themselves in their personal and spiritual development. Dance offers an alternative medium of exploration and expression, with its own unique body-language of movement, gesture, pattern and rhythm. In a culture which is bombarded by words and which prizes the cerebral over the physical, the discovery of the medium of dance can be immensely liberating and exhilarating. It can be a powerful and creative medium for exploring, accepting and affirming the whole person.

Dance can play a special rôle in the personal development of those who find acceptance of their physical self difficult: the self-conscious teenager, the physically handicapped person, the unattractive and physically inept. For the Christian, dance is a way of acknowledging the essential goodness, wonder and creativity of the human person, and of offering the self back to the creator.

Where the primary aim of the dance workshop is to promote personal and spiritual development there are a number of consequences. First, the workshop should be open to all: young and old, male and female, the agile and the fragile, the learner and the accomplished. No one need be excluded. Second, the workshop should be 'open-ended', that is to say there should be no pressure to produce or perform movement at the end of the session. The value of the enterprise is in the discovery itself, although there may be something to share with a wider audience at the end of the day. Third, what is created in the workshop need not be, and probably will not be, technically proficient or polished. The dance is successful if individuals have discovered something useful for themselves.

The second aim of the dance workshop is to enable teenagers and adults to prepare movement to share with the whole worshipping community. Dance offers an alternative medium for the exploration and expression of the church's worship. Through dance the church can express its joy, thanksgiving, praise and penitence; in dance the church can celebrate its healing, renewal and reconciliation. The language of dance can bring a rich new dimension to the worship of the church, both for those who dance and for those who watch.

Where the primary aim of the dance workshop is to prepare movement for the church's formal worship, different consequences follow. First, the workshop may *not* be open to all; a certain basic level of physical co-ordination and skill may be required. Second, the workshop will be more tightly structured and directive. Third, what is created by the group needs to communicate not only to the dancers themselves, but to the wider congregation. The dance does not necessarily need to be highly skilled and technically proficient, but it should be competent, confident, sure and strong.

Preparation

Before we could go along to conduct the workshop at St Andrew's church, we needed to spend three or four weeks preparing the ground.

First, space! Simon sets off to check out the hall we have been given, with a check-list which includes floor space, seating, number of rooms available, temperature, availability of lighting, hi-fi equipment and so on. We have learnt from previous experience that churches and church halls are often ill-equipped for movement and some improvisation is often required.

Second, time! Margaret makes a series of telephone calls to negotiate the available time. We prefer to have a series of sessions with the same group, so that there is time for getting to know each other and trying out different kinds of dance. Still, it is surprising what can be done in a single day, or even a single morning.

Third, the clientele! Carolyn and Nicky meet the organisers of the training day. How many people are they expecting? What ages will they be? Have they any experience of liturgical dance? What will they be expecting?

Fourth, ideas! Once we have a notion of what the organisers want, we can begin to plan ideas for the workshops. During several planning sessions we think through things we have done in the past and discuss new possibilities. We try ideas out, argue, laugh, work together. Gradually a structure for the workshops emerges.

Finally, resources! The final stage of planning is to gather the resources we need. Margaret will make a tape of music for exercises. Simon will prepare a tape of music for the dances. Gina will bring a stock of coloured scarves, skirts, shirts and ties for costumes. Nicky will type and duplicate passages of scripture and some canticles. Carolyn will bring bibles and blankets for the exercises.

Workshops

9.00 a.m. We arrive at the 1970s purpose-built church, hall and rooms. We are greeted by one of the organisers and shown to the large hall which we have been allocated. We now have an hour to unpack our things, limber up and pray through the day's work.

10.00 a.m. Pathfinders and their leaders are arriving. We all gather in the church for a welcome, a short service of prayer and song, and the task of choosing the day's activities. Participants mill around reading the posters advertising the workshops and signing themselves up. We stand by the dance poster to answer people's questions and to entice them to our workshops. Simon persuades a lad of fifteen to sign up!

10.30 a.m. The first workshop begins. We have fifteen dancers: mainly girls aged between twelve and fifteen, but there are two leaders aged around thirty-five and fifty-five and Simon's brave recruit. This is the group concerned with personal and spiritual development, rather than specifically preparing something for the service.

Margaret begins the session by asking everyone to introduce themselves and to say what they hope to gain from the workshop. She writes on a large sheet of paper some of the key words and phrases emerging from the group: 'finding out about dance', 'learning new dances', 'ideas for Pathfinders', 'how to start a dance group' are some of the hopes expressed. We will return to these later.

The introduction is brief so that Simon can get us moving as soon as possible with fifteen minutes of limbering up exercises.

We stretch, run and jump, to pop, folk and jazz. We learn simple breathing techniques. We split into pairs for 'mirror exercises' and 'balancing exercises'. In larger groups we learn trust and relaxation games. We end with simple yoga techniques of relaxation. As we lie, relaxed and silent, on our blankets, Simon directs attention to each part of the body which is systematically tensed and relaxed, until the whole body is limp, heavy, fluid. We enjoy a few minutes utter stillness.

Now that we are relaxed and loosened up, we begin to explore and develop a simple language of gesture and movement. We sit kneeling or cross-legged in a circle, facing inwards. Nicky leads the group in some simple choruses and Taizé chants, with very simple gestures: lifting of the head, raising and extending of the arms, bowing of the head, kneeling and curling up. After we have danced the songs once or twice, Nicky stops and begins to ask the group about the gestures they have used. We take each movement separately, slowly, and try to say what it expressed and why. We sit crouched, heads slumped on our chests. Slowly we lift our heads and extend the shoulders back until the head is high, neck stretched and free. How does this feel? Someone suggests "a feeling of release, openness". "Like being lifted out of a pit," says Sharon. "It's like a flower opening up," offers Lizzie. "I wanted to get up and run!" says Carolyn. Some are shy and hesitant, but no one is forced to speak. Gradually the sharing of our experience of movement helps us to develop a sensitivity to the language of our bodies.

Next, we begin to develop the simple gestures into more complex movements. Using the same songs and chants we begin to move, using our whole bodies to make the gestures. We try different 'shapes': dancing in one circle, two circles, a column, a semi-circle of pairs. Then we try the dances 'in canon', splitting the group into two smaller groups, singing and dancing the simple movements in canon. Individuals make suggestions and share reactions. The group begins to come alive with a sense of discovery, learning, excitement.

Next Gina splits the whole workshop into smaller groups of threes for short, simple tasks of improvisation. Each group must improvise its own movements to a range of different stimuli: emotions, like fear, anger and joy; a few short phrases of music;

different colours, red, white, yellow; a line or two from scripture. After working for fifteen minutes the groups come together and share what they have created.

Now Carolyn leads the group in teaching one of the dances we have choreographed: a simple circle dance to the Caribbean Lord's prayer. First, the five leaders perform the dance. Next Carolyn takes the group through the steps. Then the group dances it several times until they are relaxed and enjoying the movements. Afterward, we ask for comments and reactions. Someone asks if we can perform the dance in the evening celebration. The group discusses this possibility. Paul and Sue drop out; the rest of the group are excited by the idea. They dance it through once more, while Carolyn makes a few final suggestions about timing and posture. They agree to meet again at 7 o'clock for a final run-through.

12.10 p.m.   Margaret draws the workshop to a close by gathering us in an informal circle and leading an evaluation session. We go back to the jottings we made earlier to see if expectations had been met. "I'm surprised how easy I found it to dance," says Ann, who had not tried before. Paul admits that he felt self-conscious, but thinks he will try again. "Can I come back this afternoon?" asks Sharon. The feedback is helpful for leaders and participants.

12.25 p.m.   Finally we spend five minutes in silence, with individuals offering short thoughts or prayers if they wish. We close with a simple dance to the grace.

12.30 p.m.   We break for lunch.

2.00 p.m.   The afternoon workshop starts up after lunch. This time we have a smaller group of ten females: eight teenagers and two young leaders in their twenties and thirties. Several of the group have danced in church before and are keen to create some movement for the evening service.

After introductions and exercises as before, the remainder of the time is spent working on the movement for the celebration. We begin to outline ideas and possibilities, sharing material we have brought which could be worked on. Simon reads a shortened version of the Benedicite, the great Song of Creation with the repeated phrases, 'Bless the Lord ... sing his praise and exalt him for ever'. Simon explains how we might work on movement to the spoken word. The five leaders dance one of our own dances to Psalm 100, which we recite as we dance to show the group how it can be done. Margaret plays a folk setting of the Gloria, rhythmic and joyful, and suggests ways we might work on that. Nicky plays some Taizé chants and leads the group in simple movement.

Talking through this material, the group is excited by the different possibilities and decides to split into two. Half will work with Simon and Carolyn on the Benedicite, while the rest work with Margaret, Gina and Nicky on the Taizé chants.

Simon and Carolyn begin their work on the Benedicite by reading the canticle through. The group experiments with different ways of using their voices to chant this canticle of praise. They begin to try out movements for each line, working through the text. They experiment, rejecting some ideas and accepting others, until gradually a pattern emerges. A simple movement is created for the recurring refrain 'Bless the Lord'. Individuals within the group work on different movements for the verses, exploring the moods suggested by sun and moon, rain and dew, frost and snow, whales and birds. A dance is born.

Margaret, Gina and Nicky begin their work on the Taizé chants by listening to the simple melodies repeated over and over: *Veni Creator Spiritus, Veni Creator Spiritus*. The group joins in, singing the chants, praying the prayers. Nicky suggests that they work in twos or threes to develop simple movements to the repeated refrain. Then they share their ideas and decide to use two basic movements created by two of the groups. They experiment with these two basic movements in different dance formations: circles facing inward and outward, a large triangle, a simple cross, a canon. Eventually they choose the formation they like most. A dance is born.

3.50 p.m. The two groups come together to share what they have created. A few final changes are made. There is excitement and a sense of achievement. We discuss costumes: the group working on the Benedicite decides to wear tee-shirts and skirts of the same primary colour; the Taizé dancers choose white shirts and jeans, with a splash of coloured scarves.

4.15 p.m. We finish with evaluation, discussion, silence and prayer. We are tired, but excited and happy; we have created and shared something beautiful.

Celebration

After a shared meal, the dancers are ready at 7.30 p.m. in their simple costumes to contribute to the evening celebration. During the course of the day the church has been transformed into a festival of colour, movement and sound. The walls display posters, paintings, collages, poems, psalms. From the ceiling hang mobiles and banners. The music group plays jazz, folk, rock.

Candles are lit and the service begins. During the celebration groups offer what they have created during the day. We listen to scripture readings woven into a symphony of sound by different mixtures of voices. We sing a simple setting of the psalm created by the music group. The drama group offers its version of the parable of the talents. Poems are read, prayers are prayed; silence is kept. And the dancers share their dances.

The Benedicite is a great shout of praise and colour. The dancers circle round. Individuals dance to the praise of the verses: 'Bless the Lord all rain and dew ... all winds that blow ... light and darkness'. The movement of the winds, the force of the rain, the contrasts of night and day are caught up in the repeated refrain 'Sing his praise and exalt him for ever', which is danced and chanted by the whole group. The dancers are caught up in the joyful refrain, heads high, bodies moving freely; their joy is shared by us all.

The Lord's prayer is simple and short. During the prayers the dancers make their way to the altar. They are shy and awkward as they wait for the music, but as they begin to move there is ease, lightness, laughter. The tune is rhythmic; the congregation watches, prays and taps its feet. The dancers' bodies pray and celebrate.

The prayers end with the Taizé chants. The dancers are spread throughout the church, in the sanctuary and down the aisles. As the chant begins, a group of dancers takes up the prayer, begins to move, *Veni Creator Spiritus*. A second group repeats the same movement as the first moves on to the next. The movement ripples down the aisle, *Veni Creator Spiritus*. A third group takes up the movement and the prayer; then a fourth, until the whole church ripples and flows with the dancers' movements, the bodies' prayers. *Veni Creator Spiritus*: the Spirit is here!

Conclusion

The dance workshop is just a beginning. Afterwards teenagers go home to their own groups and parishes. Perhaps they share ideas, perhaps they teach a dance to others and share it in their church's worship, perhaps they set up their own groups, perhaps they find a new way of praying, of celebrating, of being. The dance workshop is just a beginning.

13 MUSIC

David Lankshear

Context

Canvey is both an island and an expanding area of new housing development. It lies in the north of the Thames estuary, about forty minutes commuting distance from London, Fenchurch Street station. In the last thirty years the population has risen from 3,000 to 36,000.

There are three Anglican places of worship on the island and these are now organised as a team ministry, with a staff of four full-time clergy. The largest of the three churches is St Nicholas', built in the 1960s. There are three services each Sunday at St Nicholas', as well as a large number of baptisms, weddings and funerals. Since the majority of these occasional offices, as well as the two main Sunday services, require music, the organist's post has been a very demanding one.

The main worship at St Nicholas' is eucharistically based. As a reflection of the needs of the congregation, most of the services follow a modern format and a variety of hymnody is provided by three different styles of hymn book: *Hymns Ancient and Modern Revised*, *100 Hymns for Today* and *20th Century Folk Hymnal*.

My family and I moved to live on the island in 1975 when I was appointed headteacher of the church school and we continued to live there for a while after I joined the diocesan staff. I had been worshipping at St Nicholas' church for five years or so when the organist resigned.

Musical resources

The first I knew of the organist's resignation was a 'phone call from the rector. The conversation went something like this.

"David, John has resigned as organist. Have you got any ideas?"

"No, not really."

"I can't think of anyone to take over as organist."

"No, neither can I."

"Could you run the choir?"

"But I don't play the organ or piano."

"Yes, I know, but you used to do the music at the school; and if I don't find someone quickly the choir will fold up."

What could I say to that? My two children were members of the choir. My wife and I both boosted the numbers on occasions and we sang in special events at the church, like performances of Handel's *Messiah* or compline sung to plainsong chants. Like the rector, I was reluctant to see the choir fold up, but I was far from convinced that I was the right person for the job. My musical skills were not those of the traditional church organist and choir master. I agreed to do it, on a temporary basis only, until someone better qualified could be found to take over.

"Good," said the rector, "I'll see you at the choir practice on Friday evening. And perhaps we could have a chat about the choice of hymns and what we are going to sing for the confirmation."

"But ...."

"Look, David, everyone will be grateful to you for taking the music on. No one will expect you to keep all the traditional music going. Just do what you can."

"But ...," I thought. It was no good. I had let myself in for it. Where on earth should I start?

The first thing I discovered is that there is a lot of musical talent available, if you are forced to look for it and if you do not make impossible demands. A large number of people sing or play musical instruments and can even enjoy doing both. Others may be willing to help organise, keep things tidy and make sure that young choristers come out of the vestry looking reasonably smart. The problem is to find these people, listen to what they are willing to contribute and then to share the responsibilities.

The second thing I discovered is that there were several people living on Canvey Island who could play the organ, although by no means all of them were regularly attached to a church congregation. Some organists keep their talent hidden, for fear lest they are expected to give up every Sunday for two services, every Friday evening for a choir practice and most Saturdays for weddings. Once they realised that this was not a real danger, they were willing to take their place on a rota. A rota of organists was the most urgent need and this proved surprisingly easy to arrange. It was soon running smoothly, with my guitar being kept in reserve or for those occasions when a guitar is a more suitable accompaniment than an organ. Only once did I have to go home to fetch it because the appointed organist failed to appear.

A further problem which remained to be solved was that of a keyboard player for choir practice on Friday evening, since my voice and guitar could not give the essential support needed by the choir as they were learning new melodies and harmonies. The solution emerged in the shape of a student at the local sixth form college. She was prepared to come to play, partly because she was interested in the experience of that strange type of playing necessary to accompany choirs. This, too, was her first real link with a church; soon she was swelling the ranks of the choir on some Sundays.

Having set up a rota of organists and found someone to play for choir practices, we could have left the matter there, but that would have ignored the vast pool of musical talent available to the church. Why should only organists be thought to have something to contribute to the worship of God? The crisis induced by our organist's resignation could be used to bring to light pianists, violinists, flautists and recorder players, to name but a few. To begin with, over half of the young people in the choir were learning an instrument of some sort. This should not have been a surprise, for so many children have the opportunity to make their first steps towards learning an instrument while they are at primary school. Moreover, the specific opportunity to play their musical instruments brought other young people into contact with the church, who otherwise had no direct link with us. Not all of these young musicians can play everything from *Hymns Ancient and Modern Revised* at first sight. Almost all of them benefit from plenty of notice, so that they can have time to practise.

It seemed right that all of these instrumentalists should have the opportunity to offer their worship to God through the talents which he had given them and which they had developed in their secular lives. The principle, therefore, of searching out the available musical talent and then enabling it to be used in public worship was the one which we applied at St Nicholas'. As the music was chosen for different services, so I began to look for opportunities to vary the musical accompaniment and so to use the various instrumental talents. It is, of course, important to match instrument with song and occasion. You do not accompany the *Old Hundredth* on a penny whistle, if there is a choice, nor do you pair *Lord of the Dance* with a French horn.

Gathering singers was also fairly straightforward. There was already the nucleus of a children's choir, mainly but not exclusively girls. A few adults also helped out on occasions and for special services. Some of these became more regular. After one or two ups and downs the numbers in the choir began to grow.

Making music should be fun. The gradually increasing flow of recruits to the choir was an indication that they at least were seen to be enjoying themselves. The institution of a choir outing also helped to make the young choir members feel that they were important and at the same time the outing helped others to take notice of the choir. When some money became available in the parish, this was spent on replacing pre-war cassocks and crumbling music copies. Again this added to the feeling that the musical side of the church was being valued.

Thus, in a relatively short space of time, we gathered together a variety of people to contribute to the musical element of the worship. The post of organist had been filled by six organists, a pianist, a variety of other players and a musical director. This may sound rather excessive, but we all found that we had plenty to do. So perhaps it is a fair indication that too much was being asked of our previous organist.

Choosing music

There is a very rich tradition of music within the Christian church. Successive generations have sought to express their faith with song and musical instruments. Our present traditions were all new music at one time. A church which is developing its musical life must be sensitive both to the traditions of the past and to the possibilities for the future. We decided at St Nicholas' that we needed to find room for some new music, thus adding to the richness of the church, while not discarding the best of the traditions we had been given. Thus, we tried to choose good music from a wide range of material.

The first clue to getting the music right is to plan well in advance, so as to know who was going to be playing what for which services. This gives the musicians plenty of opportunity to practise new material and it also gives the musical director the opportunity to select the most appropriate musicians for the occasions. It is, for example, poor management to ask musicians to play music which requires them to perform constantly at the limits of their ability.

Sometimes it can be extremely difficult to find hymns which say the right things for a particular service, or music which conveys the appropriate mood to accompany the words. A lot of time can be taken hunting through the musical archives. We should always keep in mind, therefore, that there is another practical alternative, namely to write our own material. Again churches may contain young musicians who are willing and able to give considerable time and energy in this way. For example, while I have been preparing this chapter, my teenage daughter has written her own song, taught it to others and on Sunday we will sing it as part of a pre-Christmas service. This is a tradition within church music which should not be overlooked, for without it we would not have carols like 'Silent Night'.

Advanced planning not only gives the musicians and the choir the opportunity to practise the music, it also gives them the time to think about the words. At choir practice there was time to practise each hymn, and sometimes to talk about its meaning, or indeed its story. I suspect that there is now a group of people on Canvey Island, who cannot sing a Wesley hymn without thinking about him riding round the country on his horse composing it as he went. At least they now know how the ryhthmic feel of the music should be.

It was soon apparent that some of the young people in the choir knew very little about the services they were attending, usually the eucharist. Thus choir practice became a useful occasion in which to introduce some teaching on the communion service. The adult members, far from resenting this direct teaching, actually appreciated it. Once when I apologised to them after the young people had gone home, they said "we are learning a lot" and asked for this teaching to be continued. Why is it that we assume that all the adults in our churches actually understand what we are doing during public worship?

It is often said that church congregations complain about new music. Of course, people like to sing the hymns they know. But it is not novelty, so much as unfamiliarity, which irritates a congregation. We wanted, therefore, to give the congregation the opportunity to become familiar with new music, well in advance of first expecting them to sing it. New melodies can be introduced during the music played before the service begins or as people go out. New words can be introduced as choir anthems. Often we deliberately used the period after the choir had received communion to sing material which was new to the congregation and which we were planning to ask them to participate in more fully at a later time.

Civic Service

There are two occasions in the church life of Canvey Island when the church works with the local council to produce an act of celebration. One of these is the annual civic service held in St Nicholas' church; the other is a festival of carols, held in the local community centre.

Traditionally the civic service tends to be a hymn sandwich, with all the hymns drawn from the repertoire of *Hymns Ancient and Modern Revised*. The organ plays grand cathedral music and a few tired children, forced out for a mid-week evening service, lead the singing. This year we determined to try to make the civic service more interesting musically and to involve as many people as possible. This gave the choir the opportunity to learn some new music and also enabled us to invite in some extra musicians for the occasion.

Most of the choir came to the civic service this year and for some reason they did not look as tired as in past years. The choir started the service by singing an introit chosen from a collection of modern settings written in a simple traditional style. The chosen introit focused attention on the joy of coming into church for worship, with the words 'I was glad when they said, "Let us come into the house of the Lord"'.

The three congregational hymns were all chosen from *Hymns Ancient and Modern Revised*, partly for their appropriateness to the theme and partly for their familiarity. This was important, because it enabled the whole congregation to participate in the singing, if they so wished. These hymns were also accompanied in the traditional way by the organ, which provided a firm link with past years.

This left two other prominent points in the service when music was needed, in addition to the music after the service itself was ended. From the range of options available, we decided to use a hymn from the *20th Century Folk Hymnal* accompanied on the guitar, but with the melody played on the cello by one of our young people. There were one or two raised eyebrows in the pews when I appeared in cassock and cotta, with a guitar strung round me, but, after the initial shock, the congregation responded well. The melody was played through first and then the congregation joined in. The combination of stringed instruments changed the feel of the singing and created a more reflective mood which matched the words of 'Let all that is within me cry, "Holy"'.

The other point at which music was needed provided an opportunity for a small recorder group to play, again with guitar accompaniment. On this occasion, it was a group drawn from children in the church, but it could, and perhaps should, have been a group from a local school. The final song was the round 'Shalom', sung by the choir at the end of the service: 'Peace till we meet again'.

None of this was musically complicated or adventurous, but it did provide variety and the chance for several people to contribute in their own special way to that civic service.

Festival of Carols

While most of the musical resources for the civic service came from within the congregation of St Nicholas', the Festival of Carols involves a number of other musicians, both from the other churches on Canvey Island and from non-church groups. The Festival of Carols is held in the local community centre because there is no church on Canvey Island big enough to contain it.

Preparation needs to begin long before Christmas. A special ecumenical working group is appointed from the local churches to co-ordinate the planning. While some aspects of the festival are varied from year to year, many of the features remain similar in order to build up a sense of continuity.

The musical accompaniment for the congregational singing is always provided by one of the local bands, who also play at the beginning and end of the festival. One year this might be the Salvation Army band; another year a secular group, like the town's silver band. The choirs of the local churches combine to lead the singing. This would also give an opportunity for the local choral society or Townwomen's Guild choir to join in. The principle which guides the choice of music for congregational singing is very simple. It is assumed that everyone comes for a good sing, so the congregational carols are traditional and conservative. We know the discontent which would be caused by missing out the old favourites!

In addition, each year a local school is invited to make a contribution. The schools are given total freedom to contribute in any way they choose. Some schools have provided a choir to sing less well-known carols; some have performed parts of their Christmas or nativity play; others have played original music written for the occasion. They have brought their school orchestras and recorder groups. Sometimes the musicians are young and inexperienced; sometimes they are experienced veterans of fifteen; but always they perform with joy and enthusiasm.

The balance between the traditional and the new, between the solid sounds of the brass band and the enthusiasm of the children never fails to provide an enjoyable evening and an opportunity for the churches on Canvey Island to present the Christmas message to some who might not otherwise hear it.

Conclusion

The experience of observing the transformations at St Nicholas' after the organist resigned taught me a great deal.

First, I came to recognise the abundance of musical talent, both within the church and within the neighbouring community. If you are going to give music a full place in the worshipping life of the church, it is not just a job for one person. Many people need to be involved. This is good in itself, for it enables more members of the church to offer what they have to the glory of God. It also provides opportunities for other people to become involved in the life of their local church, perhaps for the first time.

Second, I came to recognise that there is a large variety of good music from different musical traditions available for us to enhance our worship. To make good use of this variety of music, it is necessary to find people with a range of experience and understanding, in order to maximise the value of it. We need a variety of music-making groups in a large church to represent the range of musical skills in the community and to give everyone the opportunities they need. These groups must be of equal status, with no false hierarchy between the established church choir of male voices and a new group singing folk songs accompanied by a guitar.

Third, for a variety of music to flourish in a church, someone has to be clearly responsible for planning and co-ordinating it all. The key to success seems to lie in the creation in the new post of musical director. The musical director does not have to be able to play the organ, nor does he or she have to attend all the funerals, weddings and baptisms. But the musical director does need to keep a firm finger on the musical pulse of the church, at choir practice and at the majority of Sunday services. The musical director also needs to be fully alert to the musical resources of the local community in the schools and in adult groups.

Perhaps our target should be to reproduce in the minds of our worshipping community the reaction of one four-year-old on Canvey Island. The congregation and musicians had so combined that they had filled the church with the glorious sound of one of the great harvest hymns, sung uninhibitedly. Into the silence that followed the final chord, a small voice piped, "That was a good sing!"

14 SPEECH AND DRAMA

Katherine Musson

Context

Thurlby is a village of about 1,500 inhabitants, near Bourne, Lincolnshire, situated just off the main Peterborough to Sleaford road. The village has a mixed population. On the one hand, there are still some old established residents, several family names persist and farming remains a significant occupation. On the other hand, with the building of a large estate, a more mobile population has also emerged. In particular, Thurlby has attracted quite a number of teachers who commute from the village to work in neighbouring schools. (Someone counted teachers instead of sheep one night and reached forty before she could get to sleep!)

The ancient parish church goes back to the Saxon period. It is dedicated to St Firmin, a Spanish saint who became Bishop of Amiens in Northern France and who was beheaded for his beliefs during the reign of the Emperor Diocletian at the end of the third century. There is also a very active Methodist chapel in the village. On occasions such as Remembrance Sunday, Good Friday, special services and an annual 'Link Day', with a joint meal and activities, the two churches unite together.

Our exploration of speech and drama in the services at St Firmin's began when the Sunday school had dwindled to eight: the children of the two helpers, plus two others. We decided that the time had come to close the Sunday school and to start a new venture.

Our first step was to form a worship committee to think things through. We started by trying to identify the ways in which the existing Sunday school had failed in its task. It was not simply the problem that the Sunday school was going through a bad phase and failing to attract sufficient children. The problem seemed more fundamental than that. By having a separate existence from the main life of the village church, the very nature of the Sunday school seemed to invite parents to send their children along, but to stay at home themselves. At the same time, there was no natural progression for the children to graduate from Sunday school to attend Sunday church services. At that certain age, when they felt that they had become too old for Sunday school, the children seemed to lose touch with the church altogether.

Having identified the problem, the worship committee tried to think of ways in which children, preferably with their parents, could be involved in the actual worship of the church. Our original plan was to organise a non-eucharistic Family Service on the first Sunday of alternate months, taking the place of Matins held on the first Sunday of the other months, and to do something 'special' for the first part of the Parish Communion on festivals, such as Mothering Sunday and Harvest. Speech and drama quickly became core components for both the Family Services and the festivals.

Worship Committee

The formation of the worship committee provided the inspiration and the energy for our new pattern of worship. The planning and execution of these services still rests in the hands of this committee. At present the committee consists of seven people, each with different interests.

John has four children, with ages ranging from four to eleven. He brings to the committee his experience of Sunday school teaching and youth club work. He is also an expert on lighting.

Heather has two children, aged ten and thirteen. Her special interests are in dance and acting.

Evelyn has five children, one still a teenager and the others grown up. She runs the local brownie pack and guide company and so acts as a link between the worshipping community and these uniformed groups.

Heather has three children, aged two, four and five. She trained as an infant teacher and so is able to bring to the committee expertise and ideas for working among the younger age group.

Ronnie is one of the churchwardens and so provides a very useful link between the Parochial Church Council and the committee. He is also a very good actor and one of the few members of the church who does not mind learning lines.

Austin is a professor in Latin American studies living in the village. He brings a much wider and more varied experience to bear when making suggestions.

I am the seventh member of the committee, with an interest and enthusiasm for writing plays and other material for use in church. I also act as a general co-ordinator for the committee.

The worship committee has the full backing and support of the vicar and all the suggestions are discussed with him. However, the vicar does not usually attend the meetings. This gives the committee a good deal of freedom in its decisions.

While the planning of the Family Services and the festivals begins with the worship committee, we are keen to involve as many other individuals and parish groups as possible. We are an ordinary village congregation; there are few people who are in any sense skilled actors and only about a half a dozen people willing to learn many lines. We have learnt, therefore, to tailor our requirements to make the best use of the skills which are available to us. While we might find it difficult to recruit a cast of actors, there are plenty of volunteers for reading solo voices and for chorus parts.

I remember well the mistake I made as a teenager in a small village church, when I wrote and produced my first nativity play. On the great day, everyone who had a major speaking part was ill and my long-suffering sister was left with four concurrent parts. This experience taught me the advantages of giving the words to a narrator who is much more easily replaced at the last minute.

In order to illustrate how the worship committee has encouraged the development of speech and drama in the services at St Firmin's church, I shall describe just three occasions in some depth: Passiontide, Christmas and an ordinary Family Service when we worked on the theme 'Out of darkness, light'.

Passiontide

Good Friday is the main occasion each year when we develop drama in St Firmin's church. The first year we produced a published play, Edward Mürch's *No Name in the Street*. We adapted the play slightly to reduce the amount of text to be learnt, but even so there was nearly a rebellion afterwards. Far from finding the play spiritually edifying, many of the cast found the task of remembering their lines completely nerve racking.

As a result of this experience, we attempted the next year to tackle something considerably less taxing, but probably more effective. We decided to take the Passion story directly from the Gospels. The first year we used St Matthew's and St Mark's accounts; the next year we embarked on St John's account. Thirty-four members of the congregation took part in presenting St John's Passion. We tried to create different atmospheres by using different effects.

For example, the Lazarus scene in St John's gospel took place with the crowd blocking the entrance to the Lady chapel. The actual 'raising of Lazarus' was conveyed solely by a significant pause and then a bright light shining from the direction of the tomb. The atmosphere was emphasised by the amazed and awed gasps from the onlookers and by the sceptical remarks of those hostile to the miracle.

The Palm Sunday crowd assembled at the back of the church, each member carrying a branch from the yew tree which grows in the churchyard. Three or four people acted as cheer-leaders. Their exclamations, "Here comes Jesus!", "Let's make a carpet for him to walk on", "Blessings on him who comes in the name of the Lord", were echoed by a chorus of "Hosanna!".

The procession with Jesus walking in its midst passed down the centre aisle of the church, to be met by 'the opposition', two vociferous Pharisees, who changed the atmosphere of excitement and jubilation to one of doubt and indignation. The main problem here was that the crowd tended to react like naughty children when the headmaster enters the room! It took a lot of effort to persuade them to shout a defiant 'Hosanna!' and to continue the excitement, despite the rough words from the Pharisees.

The noise of the Palm Sunday crowd was then followed by the

E

quiet, calm scene of the feet washing, enacted while a quartet sang 'Bread of the world in mercy broken'.

The scene in the Garden of Gethsemane was enhanced by dim lighting, while a solo voice sang 'Hear thou my weeping' by Handel. The atmosphere was then broken harshly by the crowd coming to arrest Jesus.

Peter's observation of the scene outside in the courtyard led on to a dance by some of the children. The dance culminated in the children turning to look at Peter and one by one they pointed their fingers in his direction. There was a pause. The cock crowed and Peter broke dramatically through the children to weep at his denial.

Pilate's scene took place at the font. The crowd, urged on by the High Priest and led by the soldiers, jostled Jesus down the centre aisle for the confrontation. The action took place at the font partly to emphasise the irony of Pilate's washing his hands of the whole affair and partly to give the congregation near the back a chance to see what was going on. It was here that our drama suddenly came adrift: Pilate was the one person to forget his words and all the scripts were at the other end of the church. The narrator, however, quickly came to the rescue and valiantly folded up the scene; the singers stood and the quick thinking organist played over the opening bars of 'O sacred head': all was well again.

The crucifixion scene, we decided, would be most effective if the three crosses were clearly in view, lit from behind with dim red floodlights. Jesus was completely off stage, or to be more accurate, up a ladder in the side chapel, projecting his voice like mad. The main action focused first on the crowd. Then Mary took the centre of attention as, supported by John, she walked slowly down the centre aisle. Finally, Pilate came to the forefront. He stood gazing up at the cross after everyone else had left, to be met by Joseph of Arimathaea and Nicodemus.

This kind of presentation of the Passion required some careful preparation by the key participants. We needed to practise the central drama many times in order to achieve the best use of space and lighting and to discover or to create the desired effects. Many of the crowd, however, slotted in after just two practices. In fact the main work was in designing and rigging up the lighting and in co-ordinating the production. It was certainly a valuable experience for all who took part and the ages of the participants ranged from seven to seventy-five.

Christmas

Each year, on the Sunday before Christmas, we hold a Christingle service, based on the old North European tradition. The name means Christ-Light. The Christingle itself is an orange which represents the world. On top of the orange is a candle representing the Light of the World and around the candle are nuts and fruit symbolic of the fruits of the earth. A red ribbon around the middle of the orange symbolises the blood of Christ. Towards the end of this service, there is the Christingle procession: the children process round the church, carrying lighted candles embedded in an orange, while carols are sung.

Within this framework, we have been able to use a number of different ideas, involving groups of children and adults. Each idea has had to be simple and to include a good deal of narration and mime. We have tried to do something rather different each year.

One year I wrote a 'Christingle poem', each verse ending with the same phrase:

A baby called Jesus, born in the night,
to rescue mankind out of darkness to light.

The angel, Mary, Joseph, the shepherds, the kings, the star and all the rest of the nativity cast processed from the back of the church to the front, said a verse of the poem and then formed a nativity tableau. A lady holding a Christingle orange said the final verse, which explained the significance of the Christingle. At this point, the children joined the tableau to sing 'The drummer boy' with percussion accompaniment.

Another year we chose the carol 'It came upon the midnight clear'. After each verse had been sung, a poem, a bible reading or a short scene followed, to emphasise the words of the carol and to point to their significance for today. For example, the second verse led to a scene where a reporter interviewed two children, asking what Christmas meant to them. The children's answers mentioned presents, food and Father Christmas. The reporter then asked a mother who retorted "I shall be glad when Christmas is over", and reeled off all the tasks she had to get through before the great day. By contrast, a 'third world character' gave a picture of despair, unaltered by the events of Christmas.

The third verse led to a scene where two children started fighting over some money which had been dropped on the floor. The narrator spoke of man fighting against man on a larger scale. Then the cubs processed down the aisle, carrying the flags of the nations which were currently at war, and laid them down at the foot of the altar.

The final verse of this carol, which sings of the Old Testament prophets' proclamation of peace, led on naturally to some of the prophecies from Isaiah, foretelling a time when all the world would live in peace together.

Another year, we decided to focus the whole service around the symbolic meaning of the Christingle. At the beginning of the service two children placed a giant plywood orange on a staging block at the front of the church. The narrator explained that the orange represented the world and then a reader read Isaiah's famous words of comfort to a world torn by division and sin: 'The people that walked in darkness have seen a great light'.

A child tied a red ribbon round the orange, symbolising the blood of Jesus shed for the whole world. The choir sang the carol 'The Infant King', which tells of the infant Jesus dreaming of his crucifixion and resurrection.

Next came the dancers dressed to represent north, south, east and west, carrying coloured sticks to symbolise the four corners of the world and the fruits of the earth. Each one danced an appropriate dance. Then the four came together to show that all nations are united in Christ and they danced to the carol 'Joy to the world for Christ is born'.

Lastly, a child brought forward the candle to place in the orange, representing Jesus, the light of the world. At this point the old Russian story of Papa Panov was enacted to show how sometimes the light of Christ shines where it is least expected. When one cold Christmas day Papa Panov, the old shoemaker, offers hospitality to the weary road sweeper and to the young mother and her child he discovers that he had in fact come face to face with Christ himself. The mother with her baby and the old road sweeper came together with the dancers at the end of the play to form a tableau suggesting a nativity scene, while Papa Panov knelt and the choir sang the carol 'The little green fir tree'.

The Christingle procession followed on from this, the completed gigantic Christingle orange forming both a background and a reminder of the symbolic significance of the service.

Out of darkness, light

The idea for this theme arose in response to an article by the Bishop of Lincoln in the diocesan leaflet. This article lamented the fact that the bible was often read in church inaudibly or without giving enough meaning to the contents, with the result that the members of the congregation simply let the words flow over their heads. We decided to put together a special evening service which would focus on the bible words themselves and enhance these words by special lighting effects and music.

The theme of light seemed an ideal one to chose, as it embraced both Old Testament passages looking forward to the time of Jesus and New Testament passages pointing to Jesus himself as the fulfilment of the prophecies.

We began the evening service with the hymn 'Thou, whose almighty word chaos and darkness heard'. Then the church was plunged into darkness, and the music 'Neptune' from *The Planets* by Holst was played to suggest formless chaos. A man read the first few verses of Genesis from the back of the church,

In the beginning of creation,
when God made heaven and earth,
the earth was without form and void,
with darkness over the face of the abyss.

After this reading, the reader moved to the front of the church, carrying a lighted candle. Another voice read the first few verses of St John's gospel,

In the beginning was the word,
and the word was with God....
In him was life; and the life was the light of men.

The theme continued by illustrating how, throughout the ages, God has shown mankind a way of turning from the darkness of doubt and despair to the light of faith and confidence in him. There followed readings from different parts of the church, each part being lit up in turn. First came excerpts from Psalms 119 and 139,

> Your word is a lantern to my feet:
> and a light to my path.
>
> The darkness is no darkness with you
> but the night is as clear as the day:
> the darkness and light are both alike.

Then came some of the well-known passages from the prophets foretelling the coming of a great light, like Isaiah chapters 9 and 60,

> The people who walked in darkness
> have seen a great light:
> light has dawned upon them,
> dwellers in a land as dark as death.
>
> Arise, Jerusalem,
> rise clothed in light; your light has come
> and the glory of the Lord shines over you.

After the psalms and prophecies, we wanted to illustrate how Jesus brought to all people the light of God's presence, both in his words and in his deeds. This part of the theme was introduced by the story from chapter 9 of St John's gospel, where Jesus heals the man born blind. This was read from the back of the church, where the light focused on the font to draw attention to the method of healing as Jesus ordered the blind man 'go and wash in the pool of Siloam'.

The healing of the man born blind in St John's gospel gives point to Jesus' proclamation that 'I am the Light of the world'. The controversy stirred up by this healing shows how much that light is rejected. The light himself was also 'despised and rejected by men, a man of sorrows and acquainted with grief'. An excerpt from Handel's *Messiah* and dim lighting emphasised the solemnity of this passage and led naturally into the Passion Narrative. Readers seated in the choir stalls read St Mark's introduction to the crucifixion,

And they led him out to crucify him....
And when the sixth hour had come
there was darkness over the whole land until the ninth hour.

After this reading, the choir sang the first two verses of 'O sacred head' and in almost total darkness the whole congregation joined in the part of the creed pertaining to the crucifixion.

This led on to the poem in Philippians chapter 2 which speaks of Jesus' death and then his exaltation by God. The reader spoke from beside the high altar which was gradually and dramatically bathed in light. The association between the image of light and the Easter resurrection reached its climax in the Easter hymn 'Come, ye faithful, raise the strain', in which the risen Christ is likened to the rising sun which dispels the winter of our sins.

Then we all knelt, as different voices spoke well-known prayers on the theme of darkness and light, concluding with the evening collect 'Lighten our darkness, Lord, we pray'. The service ended with the evening hymn 'The day thou gavest, Lord, is ended, the darkness falls at thy behest'.

The advantage of this type of service was that the bulk of the work consisted in compiling the readings and commentary and in arranging the lighting. The readers were able to practise individually and in fact needed only a couple of rehearsals together so that they knew where to stand and from whom to take their cue. The disadvantage was that obviously some parts of the church were more difficult acoustically than others, and we did not always succeed in placing the strongest voices where they were most needed.

Although on this occasion we interpreted the theme of light in an entirely biblical way, we became increasingly aware that the theme is also capable of a wider interpretation, embracing both secular uses and festivals from religions other than Christianity. We hope to develop this theme further in a future Family Service.

Conclusion

The failure of the Sunday school and its replacement by family services which make good use of speech and drama have brought four new strengths to the life of St Firmin's church.

First, the formation of the worship committee itself has provided the opportunity for much more widely based leadership in worship. The invention, preparation and conducting of services is no longer left solely in the hands of the vicar. The members of the worship committee have been encouraged to discover and to develop their own particular skills and gifts and to offer these to God as part of the on-going life of the community.

Second, a wide range of adults within the village have been involved from time to time in contributing to services in a variety of ways. The links between community and church have been strengthened. At the same time, expectations and hopes for worship have been heightened.

Third, and very importantly, children have been enabled to take a full part alongside the adult members of the congregation. This has involved not just the children of regular churchgoers, but many other village children as well, including at times the brownie pack and the guide company. Children have come to recognise that worship is so much more than just sitting quietly in church, while other people say and do things.

Fourth, the experience of speech and drama in church has begun to expand the congregation's concept of worship and spirituality. We have begun to understand that the Christian God is as much creator and lord of the body as of the mind and spirit. True worship, therefore, can be no less than the uniting of body, mind and spirit and the lifting of the whole person in praise to God.

15 POETRY AND PROSE

Nicola Slee

Context

Teaching religious education in a secondary school, I became excited by the challenge of helping my pupils to study and explore the language and worship of the Christian tradition in a creative and relevant way. I could find little existing curriculum material designed to bring alive the language and imagery of Christian liturgy for teenagers. At the same time, Leslie Francis, in his capacity as non-stipendiary priest of two rural parishes, was trying to find ways of encouraging teenage parishioners and confirmation candidates to explore the church's worship.

We decided to experiment with methods of using poetry and prose as a 'way into' the study of Christian worship in our respective situations. I had already begun to discover that judiciously selected passages of fiction, biography, journalism, poetry and prose, placed alongside explicitly religious texts, could act as creative facilitators of thought and study for my students. We discovered that similar methods could be used with small, parish-based groups. Leslie set up a small group of confirmation candidates and other interested teenagers for a series of meetings and invited me to help with the group.

In this chapter, I shall describe how we prepared and used a range of material on the theme of 'music' with this parish group. Similar methods were used and found to work in school classes.

Aims

Our basic aim in selecting our material was to bring alive the language and liturgy of the church for teenagers. In order to meet this basic aim, we defined a number of more specific objectives.

First, in selecting and using poetry and prose material, we wanted to build a bridge between the everyday world and human experiences familiar to our pupils, and the language and liturgy of the church.

Second, we wanted to help our students explore the richness, the depth and vitality of the language of Christian worship and to catch something of the power of the imagery and symbolism of liturgy.

Third, we wanted to actively involve our students in the exploration of Christian worship with a range of creative activities, discussion and reflection.

Fourth, we wanted the work and discovery of the group to be shared with the wider community of the whole church, so that our discoveries would enrich the life of the local worshipping community.

Preparation

Most of our preparation for the workshops consisted of collecting the poetry and prose material we needed and deciding how we would use it with teenagers. We began with a random search over a period of weeks for material on the theme of music. We hunted in anthologies, novels, reference books, concordances, dictionaries and liturgical texts, and gradually we amassed a file of extracts. We then began to sift through and structure our material. Eventually we evolved a series of sections exploring different aspects of music in our lives and in worship.

The first section consisted of three extracts exploring how and why music may have come into the world: C.S. Lewis' lovely description of the magic creation of the world of Narnia, a short piece by Richard Baker and a poem about rhythm by Herbert Brokering. Each of the writers suggests in his own way that from the very beginning of things music has been at the heart of our world and at the heart of human experience.

In the next two sections, called 'when music speaks' and 'when music sounds', we gathered extracts which express the power of music to arouse and communicate human feelings and longings: dread, sadness and terror, as well as joy, bliss and exaltation. A piece by James Baldwin depicts an improvised saxophone solo by a kid who "stood there, wide-legged, humping the air, filling his barrel chest, shivering in the rags of his twenty-odd years, and screaming through the horn *Do you love me? Do you love me? Do you love me?"* Another passage describes the heightened reactions of a girl listening to a Beethoven symphony: "Wonderful music like this was the worst hurt there could be. The whole world was this symphony, and there was not enough of her to listen".

After exploring the power of music as an expression of human feelings, we assembled passages which illustrate the music in the natural world: the music of birds, sea, wind, rain and animals. We found some gloriously vivid images, ranging from Pooh's 'hum', in which the honey-bees are "gumming" and "humming", to MacCaig's poem about the donkey who "gets madder every minute", trying to make a "round rich note", and only managing to produce "that whooping-cough trombone", "heehawing" and "seesawing".

In the next section, we placed extracts of scripture and hymnody and other pieces which depict creation's music as an offering to God. The Benedicite expresses this beautifully, with its long paean of praise in which sun and moon, rain and dew, light and darkness, whales and birds, beasts and cattle, priests and people, all sing God's praise 'and exalt him for ever'.

Finally, we concluded with two sections on the church's music. In the first, we collected passages which explore why music is so important in worship and reflect upon its place in liturgy. In the second we gathered descriptions of different uses of music in various kinds of worship: a Russian orthodox liturgy, Gregorian chant in a Trappist monastery, and a modern light-and-sound celebration in an American discotheque, to name but three. These extracts had one thing in common: the powerful and effective use of music as a medium of relationship between God and his people in worship.

When we had collected our material, we devised a list of activities and discussion questions to go with each section and planned the content for a sequence of meetings. After four sessions of group work, using the extracts, we planned to prepare a special Parish Communion on the theme of music.

Finally, for our preparation, we visited a number of local teenagers and invited them to the group. We made copies of the extracts for each member and gathered any resources we might need: pens and paper, bibles, music books, record player and so on. We were ready to begin!

Workshops

Workshop one   It is Sunday evening; the rectory doorbell rings at 8.00 p.m. and the group begins to arrive. Over coffee we chat informally. There are six young people between the ages of thirteen and sixteen, Katie, John, Stephen, Jennifer, Anne and Jill, and the two leaders, Nicola and Leslie. Leslie opens the workshop by outlining some of the possibilities, the shape of the workshop sessions and the idea of helping to prepare a Sunday morning service.

We begin to explore our theme with two quick brain-storming exercises. For three minutes, we jot down everything we can think of to do with 'music'. After three minutes we stop and do the same again, but now the cue is 'music in church'. After another three minutes, we pool our ideas and make two big lists. The 'music' list includes favourite songs and groups, musical instruments, voice parts, different types of music and more. 'Music in church' produces a much shorter list: hymns, psalms, organ, choir, and that's about it.

Next we try to make a list of 'a day's music', consisting of the different kinds of music we might hear in a typical day. This starts off with waking up to the sounds of birds and rain on the window, singing in the shower, radio over breakfast and so on.

Now we introduce the first extracts of poetry and prose, three pieces exploring the beginnings of music and the human need for music. We split into twos and threes, each taking one of the passages and a few questions to help us think through the material. Why is there music in the world? Why do we want or need music? What would be missing in life if there was no music? What is the writer trying to communicate about music?

After fifteen minutes we come back into the group to share our reactions. "So, why did God put a beat in everything?" prompts Nicola. "To make the world a more interesting place." "To make it a happy place." "Why does music make us happy?" "Because it is lively, energetic, because it makes you want to dance, because it makes you feel good." "Because it expresses deep human feelings that you can't put into words." "How would the world be if there were no music?" "Empty." "Quiet." "Sad." "I can't imagine a world without music—it's impossible."

We discuss C.S. Lewis' picture of creation through music. "What does it make you feel?" prompts Nicola. Jill describes a sense of excitement and mystery and others join in. "It's magic, kind of shivery." "The music is alive, it's bringing everything into being." "What is C.S. Lewis trying to convey by describing the creation in this way?" "The wonder and mystery of everything." "It's very poetic, very vivid", says Anne, "you can just picture it all happening."

We move on to the poem by Brokering. "Why is rhythm so important?" "It's what gives music the beat, a shape, you know what is coming next." We develop the idea of shape in music, our need for structure and rhythm in life. "What aspects of our lives are regulated by rhythm?" "Breathing." "Our heart-beat and pulse." "Waking and sleeping." "What about rhythm in the natural world?" "Day and night." "The seasons." "The sea and the waves make music," and so on. We are beginning to see that rhythm, shape, music are at the very heart of the world and of our human experience.

It is nearly time to stop. We add some more items to our 'music' list, including the sounds of the natural world we have just identified. Then Nicola sets the group two tasks for next week. First, everyone is asked to bring a favourite piece of music and to share it with the group, saying why they like it; second, everyone is given extracts to read for our next meeting.

To end, we read 'A Song of Creation' antiphonally, from *The Alternative Service Book 1980*. We listen to a short prayerful Taizé chant and gradually join in as the music continues to play. We say the grace and disperse.

Workshop two   We begin our second meeting with half the group sharing the music they have brought. We listen to a recent chart single, a Chopin nocturne, the theme-song from a smash American movie, some Oscar Peterson. Different reasons are given for choosing the pieces: associated memories and feelings, appreciation of technical mastery, or just sheer enjoyment.

Most of the session is spent working on the extracts the group had taken away from the previous meeting. The passages all describe the various effects of various kinds of music on different listeners. We read each extract in turn, discussing the feelings, ideas and themes. We talk about the power of music to express what cannot be said in words, the way in which music evokes particular occasions and associations, the emotional release of energy we sometimes feel when listening to music.

We listen to the music brought by the other half of the group, and then close with a psalm and prayers. We send the group away with more extracts to read and the task of finding a description of music in creation to bring back to the next meeting.

Workshop three We spend our third meeting exploring a range of extracts which conjure up something of the music of the created order: the music of birds, sea, wind, rain and the animal kingdom, seen as the creation's offering of praise to its creator. We read poems, Pooh hums, scripture and some extracts brought by the group. We build up a rich sense of the varied symphony of sound which abounds in the natural world.

We spend some time finding biblical passages which speak of worship offered to God by creation, and which call upon the Christian to offer praise to God in music. We begin to think about the way we use music in our own services. We send the group away to think about why we use music in church, and what its purpose should be.

Workshop four In this meeting we want to think more explicitly about the function of music in the church's worship. We start by asking for reactions to the question "Why do we use music in church?" The answers are mixed. "To praise God." "To express our worship." "To express our unity with each other." "It's something we can all do, not just the vicar."

We explore these ideas in a range of extracts. We discuss how the music of worship can be God-centred and God-directed, as Robin Leaver suggests. We discuss Joseph Gelineau's idea that "music should enable us to hear the unheard". After a while we start to think of specific kinds of music used in the church's worship, in different traditions. We make a list: hymns, psalms, plainsong, negro spirituals, organ music and much more.

Next we turn to the range of extracts which describe different kinds of music used in different places and traditions of the church: the antiphons, chanting and intoned readings of the Russian orthodox liturgy; Gregorian chant in a Trappist monastery; folk guitar and song in a Benedictine monastery; and an extraordinary experimental celebration in an American discotheque which includes a multiscreen light and music collage, dancing, choruses, Bach's *St Matthew Passion*, the march music from Z and the Beatles' 'Here comes the sun'.

Discussion then turns to our own church worship and music. We explore how we could change and improve the music in our own church. This really gets discussion going. There are wildly improbable suggestions: hiring an orchestra, using a rock band, sacking the organist, playing disco music. Other ideas are somewhat smaller and more pragmatic in scale: learning new hymns, having a small music group to lead singing or to perform during the communion, using tapes and records in some services.

Our discussion takes us to the end of our time. We ask the group to go away and think of ideas for the service which we will be planning at our final workshop.

Workshop five   There is plenty to do in our final planning meeting to prepare for the Parish Communion. We start with a discussion of our aims. What are we trying to do in the service? "Share what we have learnt with the congregation," says Anne. "Show how music is an important part of our lives which we can offer to God," suggests Jennifer. "See how there are lots of different ways to use music in worship," Katie throws in, "and we want to try some of them out instead of always doing the same old thing". "To help the congregation worship more deeply," suggests Jill.

Now we think through each aspect of the service. What about the organisation of the building? Stephen suggests a collection of different musical instruments on a table by the entrance. "We could have records and tapes too," says Anne. We begin to make a list of artifacts that could be displayed and we plan to bring them to the altar at the offertory, as a sign of offering our musical talents to God. What about a display of pictures and written work too?

Next we plan the ministry of the word. Leslie suggests that for this, instead of the normal biblical readings and sermon, we should construct our own collage of readings and ideas. We discuss how this could be done and work out a plan. Nicola will introduce the ministry of the word by describing our work over the sessions and explaining briefly our theme. Then different members of the group will share the main ideas discussed at each of our meetings and read some of the extracts we have used. Leslie will try to draw all the ideas together in a brief summary. Katie and Jill offer to write some prayers on the theme of music.

We then turn attention to the kind of music we want in the service itself. We begin by pooling our own talents. Katie and Nicola both play the piano; Stephen is good on the guitar and Jennifer can be persuaded to play simple melodies on the recorder. As a group we can make a tolerable singing noise. We begin to experiment with some music for the communion: one or two simple choruses and Taizé chants. Then we think about the music for before and after the service. Stephen and John suggest making up a tape of different kinds of music to play while people are coming into church. We all make suggestions of short pieces to put on the tape: part of Beethoven's *Pastoral Symphony*; a song from *Jesus Christ Superstar*; a Bach cantata; a Fisher Folk version of a psalm. Stephen agrees to put together this cacophony of sound for the service. After the service we plan to use the 'Ode to Joy' from Beethoven's ninth symphony. Finally, we choose some contemporary hymns and songs to include in the congregational singing.

Eucharist

On Sunday morning our project shapes the Parish Communion. As the congregation approaches the church all appears to be as usual: John is tolling the bell to call people to worship. As they enter the porch, however, they find the walls posted with pictures of pop groups, choirs, orchestras, musicians, record sleeves and other signs of our theme. As they walk into the church they are greeted by the sounds of Beethoven, rock opera and folk music from the tape which Stephen has made. As they walk to their seat they pass a large table loaded with percussion instruments, violin, recorder, flute, music, concert programmes and more. As they survey the church they see the walls covered with signs of our work: poems, psalms and pictures celebrating our joy in music and calling the church to offer music in praise to God.

Before the service proper begins, we sing hymns and songs, led by Stephen on the guitar and percussion instruments shared amongst the group. We distribute tambourines, castanets and home-made rice-shakers among some of the children in the congregation so that they too can join in. After the opening greeting and prayers, in the ministry of the word we share with the congregation the work we have done. We explain the material displayed on the walls and comment on the different music being used in church. We read some of the extracts we discussed in the workshops. Leslie sums up our work in a brief comment or two. After the creed, we are led in prayers by Katie and Jill: we praise God for the joy of music, the richness and variety of sound in the natural world; we ask the Holy Spirit to inspire our own worship; we offer our own gifts and senses to be shared with our creator and with each other.

At the offertory some of the musical instruments, records and songbooks are brought to the nave altar and offered with the bread and the wine as a sign of our music offered to God. During the communion, the congregation is led in gentle, rhythmic chanting and simple choruses repeated over and over. There is a sense of worship, happiness, rhythm and joy. The Lord is with us; the Spirit is in our midst.

After the final hymn, there is a moment of silence and then the strains of Beethoven's 'Ode to Joy' boom out and fill the building, rising and circling up to the nave roof and filling our hearts with a tremendous sense of celebration.

Afterwards the congregation lingers in church, listening to the music, looking at the display material, talking to the young people who had prepared it all. There is a lot of comment and encouragement as well as a few grumbles from those members of the congregation who would have preferred their traditional Sunday morning service. At last we spill out into the rectory for coffee; the church settles back into its own sense of silence and peace, drawing the sounds of music back into the stillness.

Note

The anthology material discussed in this chapter, on 'the world of music', is published in *A Feast of Words* by Leslie J. Francis and Nicola M. Slee, together with three other sections on 'meetings and encounters', 'the symbol of water' and 'the presence of mystery'.

16 ADULT GROUPS

Leslie J. Francis

Context

The main emphasis of the previous chapters involved building bridges between the regular liturgy of the worshipping community and those on the fringes of the church. Often project work among children and young people has provided the central link, not only for young people, but for their parents and the local community as well. Such a strategy has inevitable consequences for the regular and faithful worshippers.

The Parish Communion has become the context for pre-school children and infants to bring their teddy bears to a picnic and to dance their teddy bear dance in the nave. Junior aged children have stuck their collages to the medieval arcades, constructed models around the font, and suspended mobiles and balloons from the rafters. Teenagers have introduced their kind of music, their kind of drama, their kind of liturgical dance and their kind of dialogue. In the name of making the liturgy more attractive to children and fringe churchgoers, we have introduced a nave altar, offertory processions and a general movement during the peace, as well as making the illustrated communion book available to all worshippers.

All of these factors have been noticed by the regular churchgoers; not all of them have been welcome all the time. Some of the regulars have been surprised; others confused and a few angry. It is, of course, crucially important to minimise this confusion and anger. A worshipping community which resents changes and resists modifying its practices to accommodate the unchurched is hardly likely to create the atmosphere of spontaneous welcome, which is so essential in making contact with those on the fringes of the church, adults and children alike.

I am convinced that if changes are to be welcomed by a worshipping community, or even positively tolerated, the reasons behind these changes have to be thoroughly discussed, thought about and understood. I have, therefore, always wanted to give considerable emphasis in the ministry of preaching to the questions of the place of children in liturgy and contact with those on the fringes of the church. I have also wanted to give the Parochial Church Council the full opportunity to debate changes before they take place and to share with me the responsibility for initiating new things. This process has slowed down all sorts of initiatives, but also has been central to their ultimate acceptability.

Sunday preaching and debate in the Parochial Church Council are certainly helpful ways of involving the regular members of the worshipping community in sharing responsibility for making contact with those on the outside of the church, but the real clue seems to lie in giving the regular worshippers opportunities to explore worship themselves in novel contexts and in novel ways. Often resistance to change stems from inadequate concepts, limited experience and insecurity in novel situations.

Central to my own understanding of eucharistically-based parish liturgy is the opportunity for regular worshippers to experience that same liturgy in the more relaxed and less formal setting of the private house. For example, a group of worshippers who are unaccustomed to the friendly informality of exchanging a sign of peace can explore this on the first few occasions more naturally and less self-consciously outside their usual environment of the formal church building. Having experienced passing the peace at an informal celebration of the communion, these same worshippers may begin to feel uncomfortable *not* doing so in the Parish Communion on Sunday. House Communions, therefore, can have a very important part to play in the development of parish worship among the regular church members, as well as providing another route of access for those not yet committed to the church.

House groups

Before discovering the House Communion, I had experienced a range of house groups, as parishioner, student and parish priest. These house groups had been formed in a number of ways, around bible passages, study topics or prayer themes. Certainly, in the relatively homogeneous student environment such groups work well. Students seem to have the ability, motivation and technique to talk endlessly on a variety of topics, whether informed about them or not.

Student Christian bodies invariably include within their number some, at least, who are familiar with issues of bible scholarship and read bible commentaries, as well as pursuing a disciplined regular pattern of bible reading. Students often have the time and resources to do their homework before a discussion group on a specific topic. Since open prayer meetings presuppose certain shared assumptions and experiences, these, too, tend to develop well in the context of student Christian bodies.

All of these qualities are, of course, important components of the vital Christian community; but they are not qualities which emerge overnight in the average parish. The mistake in a lot of parish house group work is to assume that the assumptions which hold in the Christian student environment, or the theological college, will transplant into parish life.

Certainly, I wanted to stimulate serious bible study in my small parishes, but I have been content when just one or two individuals, committed to the exercise, have met regularly to develop this skill. I wanted to stimulate discussion groups, but I have tried to be careful to invite individuals who have sufficient in common to make discussion profitable. These strategies make good educational sense; they contribute towards the religious and spiritual development of the individuals involved in them. On one view, the development of individual Christian lives can contribute enormously to the strength and resources of the parish. On another view, however, these groups can also be painfully exclusive and dangerously divisive; they can accentuate the difference between those who participate in them and those who do not.

House Communion

The House Communion, on the other hand, need not be so divisive in the same way. All of those adults who regularly participate in the Sunday Parish Communion can find themselves taking part in and enjoying their participation in the House Communion. What is crucial, however, is that the regular worshippers at the Parish Communion get the right idea about the House Communion from the very start and do not project on to it their previous images and experiences of house groups centred around the bible or study. It is for this reason that I wanted to talk about House Communions before doing them and I have also wanted to have the very first House Communion fully approved by the Parochial Church Council.

Inevitably waiting for the Parochial Church Council delayed the introduction. In one case, two particular families were reluctant to give their approval to the experiment. The first family, partly from a Presbyterian background, were cautious of seeing the parish move any further towards a eucharistically-centred tradition. The second objector was very concerned lest the eucharist, which symbolically unifies the parish at the Sunday Parish Communion, might also become a divisive act of attracting some and simultaneously alienating others if celebrated in a private house. When eventually the Parochial Church Council decided to experiment, both of these families came to the first House Communion and both went away convinced that it was an appropriate and right course of action for the parish to have followed.

The House Communion can, of course, take place in any home in the parish. It is a nice theory that every regular churchgoer's house is equally open to worshippers of the Christian community. In practice, this ideal is not always realisable. Some homes are too small; others are shared by families of unequal commitment; others need to cater for the life-style of teenage children or irregular shift work. Social demarcation, too, continues to have a powerful and debilitating part to play, even within the Christian community. In my own non-stipendiary ministry, my parsonage house has provided the appropriate environment to which parishioners have felt happy to come and where they have been able to relax. The rectory lounge has been able to combine the public openness of the church with the relaxed comfort of the private home.

The informality of the House Communion, which is one of the major strengths of the home setting, is not something which is achieved without careful preparation and planning. It is crucial to think through what is going to happen beforehand and to take care to structure the environment accordingly.

To begin with, I arrange the furniture in my lounge to create a circle or semi-circle of comfortable chairs around the perimeter of the room. I try to judge the number of chairs necessary so that there are no empty seats and I usually need to bring in a few extra chairs for those who arrive last. One small simple table is placed to mark the focal point of the room and all unnecessary furniture is removed. The front door is left ajar so that people can come in easily, but I do try to welcome them individually and to make sure that introductions are made.

When the service is ready to begin the rectory telephone is disconnected and the atmosphere is deliberately changed. As people arrive, I encourage them to talk to each other and to relax socially, but, before the service begins, I want the atmosphere to change to one of quiet reflection. On some occasions a record or tape is played for a few minutes while we listen in silence; on other occasions a repetitive Taizé chant is used. When the atmosphere is right, the service begins with the opening greeting and the collect for purity.

The presidency of the service is also carefully planned beforehand. While the ministry of the sacrament necessarily remains with the priest, the earlier part of the service is led by one lay person and the intercessions by another.

On some occasions the ministry of the word remains quite brief and sharply focused. Three lesson readers will have been selected beforehand and someone will link those three readings in a meditation or with some explicit teaching. In this way, the House Communion provides opportunities for more direct teaching than the Sunday sermon. For example, close attention can be given to specific bible passages: a range of translations of one passage can be made available to each member of the group or attention can be concentrated on the way in which the three synoptic gospels each handle the same material in different ways. In the relaxed atmosphere of the House Communion, bible study can be fun.

On other occasions the ministry of the word can become quite extended. The scriptural readings are complemented by a collage of other readings, by music and song. These readings become the basis for study and discussion. In this way a discussion group actually takes place in the middle of the communion service. Inevitably some people will not want to contribute to the discussion, but, since discussion is only one part of the evening's programme, they do not feel so excluded from the whole activity.

The intercessions are deliberately kept open-ended, so as to provide an opportunity for free prayer. Although one individual has been invited beforehand to provide some planned prayer-leads within the structure of the Rite A prayer of intercessions and thanksgivings, plenty of space is left for others to contribute. Again, some members of the group feel happier contributing in this kind of way than others; so no pressure is put on all members of the group to conform to this practice. Experience shows, however, that over a period of time the number of people wanting to contribute to the open prayer sessions and the range of issues spoken in prayer both increase.

The prayers of penitence can be used very reflectively in the House Communion. The pace of the home liturgy allows space for individuals to reflect on their relationships with God and with each other. Sometimes at this point in the liturgy we have interpolated another Taizé chant, an extended kyrie or a responsorial penitential psalm.

The peace provides the opportunity to celebrate our sense of restored relationship with God and with each other. In the context of the House Communion, the peace also serves two other practical purposes. Especially if there has been an extended ministry of the word, people will have been sitting in one position quite long enough and so welcome the opportunity for a short walk-about. Second, during the peace it is possible to move the communion table into a more prominent position, provide a white cloth and prepare the bread and wine.

Until the peace the whole of the service will have been conducted in a sitting position. As president I choose to stand for the eucharistic prayer. Usually the general feeling is that the whole group wants to stand at this point also, but I am careful to recommend a sitting position if there are members of the group who are likely to have problems with standing comfortably for this period of time.

For the administration, we stand and pass the bread and wine around the group, each person administering the sacrament to his or her neighbour by name. After receiving, we sit. Those who do not wish to receive simply let their neighbour know beforehand. Before the post communion prayer, there is again the opportunity for silence, listening to recorded music or singing. The House Communion ends with the blessing, not the dismissal. People are free to go or to stay and talk. The telephone is reconnected and life resumes at the rectory. The communion vessels and the white cloth are taken away and the coffee table reassumes its original function of receiving coffee, milk, sugar and biscuits.

Agape

Celebrating communion in the home is a powerful reminder of the institution of that sacrament in the context of the Jewish family meal held to celebrate the Passover. It is a relatively natural step, therefore, to progress from the House Communion to the rediscovery of the Agape, the celebration of communion around the supper table. The potential of the Agape has now been recognised in Anglican liturgy by the Liturgical Commission's services for *Lent, Holy Week, Easter* (1986).

Our first parish Agape was celebrated towards the end of Lent, but not on Maundy Thursday itself, since we wanted to retain our practice of an evening celebration of holy communion in church, followed by a watch into the night. What we had in mind for the Agape was made well known in advance through the Parochial Church Council, preaching and the parish newsletter. For this occasion we asked people to let us know in advance of their intention to come, to help with the catering and with the seating arrangements. The response was more encouraging than we had anticipated; trestle tables and chairs were needed from the hall.

Many of the same principles applied to preparing for the Agape as for the House Communion. Shortage of space, however, meant that people were shown to a seat at the table as soon as they arrived and once in the room they were rather locked into their place! The table was laid for a simple three course meal; service booklets and hymn sheets were placed with the side plates. When the last member of the group had arrived, we sang a well known hymn, sitting round the table.

Because the first Agape was a novel experience for the majority of those present, I followed the opening hymn with a brief, but fairly formal meditation and explanation of what we were about to do. At this stage, the only food and drink on the table were baskets of small bread rolls and bottles of red wine and red grape juice. We thought of the bread and wine as signs of physical and spiritual sustenance and as sacraments of table fellowship and Christian communion. In this context, the bread and the wine were powerful indicators of the essential continuity between the physical and the spiritual. We then gave time for the rolls to be shared around the table and the glasses to be filled. The formal greeting of the communion service was spoken and the first course of the meal was served.

After the soup/grapefruit we began the ministry of the word with the collect and the scriptural readings. On that first occasion we deliberately took as our theme the readings from *The Alternative Service Book 1980* for 'Thanksgiving for the institution of holy communion'. The leisurely pace of this part of the service allowed for some discussion of the readings. This discussion led naturally into the prayer of intercessions and thanksgivings. Again, the pace and informality of the occasion encouraged individuals to make their own contribution to these prayers.

After the intercessions, the main course of the meal was served: baked potatoes and a huge casserole which had been bubbling away all evening in the rectory kitchen. The red wine and the red grape juice continued to make their way around the table. Conversation moved backwards and forwards, in a relatively relaxed manner, between discussion related to the significance of what we were doing and all the topics of general, local and personal interest which surface when members of the local church have time to talk informally together.

The main course was followed by the prayers of penitence and the peace. Since lack of space in the rectory lounge prevented us from walking around to exchange the sign of peace more generally, we simply linked hands around the table as the peace was spoken by the whole group in unison.

The third course of the meal consisted of the small bread rolls and cheese. We finished the meal in the same way as we had started it by sharing the basket of rolls around the table and this provided a natural introduction to the eucharistic prayer. As the remaining plates were cleared away from the table the president's place received the common cup of wine and the plate for the bread of the eucharist. Now the president stood, but the rest of the group remained seated. After the eucharistic prayer the bread and the wine were passed around the table, with all members of the group administering communion to their neighbours by name. Another hymn was sung before the post communion prayer and blessing.

In place of the dismissal, people were invited to stay: to do the washing up, to load the tables into the pickup truck for the return journey to the hall and to make coffee. "Why", asked one of the regular churchgoers, who had been most reluctant to initiate House Communions in the parish, "Why haven't we experienced this kind of thing before?"

Conclusion

The House Communion and the Agape have provided opportunities for the adult regular churchgoers to experience their regular communion service celebrated in different contexts and with different emphases. This experience has given them new insights into the significance of the communion service and the confidence to welcome change and experimentation in the Sunday services.

The House Communion has also brought a number of other benefits. Members of the Sunday congregation who have not immediately felt comfortable in or able to contribute to other forms of house groups have felt welcome to attend the House Communion. By so doing, they have found themselves given opportunities for bible study, discussion and open prayer; some have remained silent, but not conspicuously so, while others have begun to participate more actively. At the same time, newcomers to the parish and those in the process of becoming more committed church members have found the House Communion a helpful form of entry into the liturgy and relationships of the worshipping community. Having made contact, the local church needs to provide opportunities for continued nurture, development and growth.

NOTES ON CONTRIBUTORS

Andrew Bowden was born in a Somersetshire village in 1938 and lived in villages in Somerset and Gloucester until his ordination in 1965. He was a curate in inner city and surburban parishes until 1972, but then returned to the country benefice of Byfield in Northamptonshire. He now ministers in a cluster of villages near Cirencester combining this with the chaplaincy at the Royal Agricultural College and a diocesan appointment as the Bishop of Gloucester's adviser on rural society. Underlying his ministry has been the belief that God works in and is concerned about secular life, and that the church should listen to the religious insights of 'the world'. He has published articles in *New Fire* and *Theology* and was co-editor of *A Second Workbook in Rural Evangelism*.

John Duckett was born in 1941 in Canterbury. He spent fifteen years as a teacher in junior schools in Suffolk, Derbyshire and Sheffield, and developed a special interest in children's writing and drama. He became an Anglican ordinand in his late thirties, was trained at Lincoln Theological College and served his title in the diocese of Lincoln at Boston. He is now in his first incumbency, a group of four rural parishes in South Lincolnshire.

Leslie J. Francis was born near Colchester, Essex, in 1947. He has pursued a dual career as a social psychologist and as a non-stipendiary parish priest. His research, concentrating on the relationship between young people and the church, includes *Teenagers and the Church* (1984), *Rural Anglicanism* (1985) and *Partnership in Rural Education* (1986). His experience as a parish priest began in an expanding town and then moved to rural parishes in Suffolk and Gloucestershire. His catechetical material, like *The Child and the Eucharist* (1980) and *His Spirit is With Us* (1981) has its roots in the experiences of these parishes. He is currently research officer at the Culham College Institute for Church Related Education in Abingdon.

David Lankshear was born in London in 1943. He has been, by turns, an articled clerk, a class teacher in primary schools, warden of a teachers' centre and headteacher of a Church of England primary school. Currently he is senior adviser for schools in the diocese of Chelmsford. He has a wife and two teenage children who share his interest in music, which is expressed by singing in the local choral society and a church folk music group, as well as in writing songs, both sacred and secular. Along with a number of articles and poems some of his songs have appeared in books and periodicals. His other interests include the development of the school curriculum, particularly religious education and mathematics, and research into the involvement of children with the church.

Katherine Musson was born in 1951 and spent her early childhood in Suffolk and Sussex, before moving up to Lincolnshire as a teenager. Having graduated from Durham University in Theology, she spent some years teaching. She has contributed regularly to the junior section of the *Church Times*, *Together* and some of the Lincoln diocesan publications for children, and has written and produced material to be performed in church. She is married to a vicar, and they have two children. Her interests include singing, dance, drama and building up family services.

Paddy Phillips grew up in Hurstpierpoint, Sussex, but since her marriage in 1962 has lived with her husband, the Revd Stephen Phillips, three children, two dogs, one cat and a variety of other people in Lincolnshire. She trained at Norwich Training College as an infants' teacher and is currently teaching part-time in a village school. During 1978-81 she completed the East Midland Ministerial Training Course in theological pastoral studies. She and her husband share a vision of the local church being a community where people of all ages and stages are encouraged to grow to their full potential in the overarching awareness of the love of God.

Nicola Slee was born in 1957 and spent her childhood in North Devon. She has studied theology and educational psychology, and currently lectures in religious studies at the Roehampton Institute of Higher Education. She has a particular interest in the rôle of literature and the arts in Christian spirituality, nurture and worship, and has a range of experience in conducting workshops and projects for children and adults on liturgical dance, prayer and spirituality, and various forms of experimental liturgy. Her previous publications include a number of articles and poems and, in association with Leslie Francis, *A Feast of Words* (1983) and *The Teddy Horsley Series for Young Christians*.

Doreen Storr was born in Louth, Lincolnshire. After training as a primary school teacher she has spent many years working with young children as a class teacher and as a headteacher. She served on the consultative committee of the Schools' Council Primary School Project on Religious Education and made a contribution to *Groundplan*, a discussion document on the aims and objectives of religious education. During this time she produced various articles for the Christian Education Movement including one in *A Dictionary of Religious Education*. The past two years have been spent as adviser for religious education in church schools and children's voluntary religious education in the diocese of Lincoln and she is currently back in the classroom teaching young children. Her latest publication is *What shall we do for Christmas?* (1985).

INDEX

adults, 23, 47, 49, 59, 65–71, 73, 92, 108–116, 120, 122, 131, 136, 147–155
advent, 52
agape, 153–155
altar, 61, 70, 82–83, 147
Alternative Service Book 1980, 32–33, 49, 53, 141, 154
Angelus, 101
anthology, 29, 137–146
assembly, 13–14, 88, 98–99
At the Lord's Table, 30–31
attitude formation, 20

Baboushka, 90
band, 29–30, 124
banners, 52, 63, 92
baptism, 38, 51, 80
benedicite, 113–115, 139, 141
bible, 14, 16, 19, 58, 111, 115, 131, 133–135, 140, 142, 149, 151
Book of Common Prayer, 32, 50
British Council of Churches, 16, 19
brownies, 127, 136
buildings, 17, 66, 74

catechism, 14
Child in the Church, The, 16, 19
choir, 24, 43, 51, 58, 118–125
choral speech, 29, 39, 69, 70, 93–96, 103, 126–136
Christian nurture, 11, 16–21, 99
Christian Union, 100–101
Christingle, 131–133
Christmas, 33, 51, 53, 86–87, 90–91, 106–107, 123–124, 131–133
church schools, 14–15, 28, 65, 81–83, 88–97, 117
civic service, 122–123
coffee, 44
collage, 48, 61, 63, 69, 70, 74–75, 77, 81, 106
Collins, T., 50
Come and Praise, 24
Come and Worship!, 38–40
communion, 20, 22–31, 32–33, 39, 48–49, 50–56, 59–61, 79–83, 84, 101–102, 106, 108, 144–145, 147–155
communion, admission to, 24
congregation, 16–18, 93, 136
cooking, 61, 62–63, 67–68, 75, 76–77, 82
crèche, 20, 23, 67

creed, 27, 37
critical openness, 19
cubs, 132

dance, 24, 29, 67, 69, 71, 81, 90, 108–116, 127, 130
death, 26, 48
drama, 29, 34, 39, 48, 52, 67, 71, 90, 106, 115, 126–136

Easter, 62–63, 77–78, 86, 105, 106
eating, 63, 69, 71, 73, 82–83, 84, 115, 153–155
ecumenism, 33–34, 39, 124, 126
Education Act 1870, 15, 88
Education Act 1944, 13–15, 88, 98
entertainment, 42
evening prayer, 32, 57, 90

family day, 28, 65–71
family service, 11, 32–40, 46, 72, 127
Feast of Words, A, 146
finance, 17–18, 43
forgiveness, 53–55
Friday club, 57–64

Good Friday, 62–63, 72–78, 129–131
guides, 40, 127, 136

harvest, 33, 59–60, 66–71
Hirst, P.H., 15, 18
His Spirit is with us, 11, 31
Holy Spirit, 27, 28–30
house communion, 40, 148–153
house group, 34, 40, 46, 148–149
Hull, J.M., 14
hymns, 14, 16, 24, 29, 34, 37, 38, 117–125

illustrations, 25–27, 38
indoctrination, 19
ink-blot, 54–55

Jenkins, P., 25
Jonah-man Jazz, 105–106

large churches, 50–56
Lent, 61–63
Lent, Holy Week, Easter, 153
Lewis, C.S., 138, 141
light, 26, 62, 68, 75, 78, 86–87, 133–136
lighting, 53, 78, 127, 129–130, 133–135
Link club, 45–46
Listen!, 77
Lord is Here, The, 30, 65

Maundy Thursday, 62–63, 77, 95
media, 42
mobiles, 62–63
morning prayer, 32, 33–34
Mothers' Union, 40
multicultural, 14, 26
music, 24, 34, 43, 53, 61, 62, 67, 68, 69, 70, 75, 77, 81, 90, 92, 104, 105–106, 115, 117–125, 130, 137–146

National Society, 88
needlework, 67, 69
neighbourhood, 26
No Name in the Street, 129

Occasionals, 42, 46–47
offertory procession, 24, 44, 55, 69, 145, 147

Palm Sunday, 91–97, 129
Papa Panov, 132–133
paper sculpture, 87, 106–107
papier mâché, 21, 34
Parochial Church Council, 12, 33, 103, 128, 148, 150, 153
Pathfinders, 108
Peace, 36, 37–38, 44, 55, 147, 148, 152, 154
Pentecost, 85
play school age, 21, 34
poetry, 137–146
pre-school age, 20, 23, 147
primary school age, 20, 22–30, 65, 73, 88–97, 147
procession, 51, 63, 92, 129, 131, 133
psychological development, 20, 24, 79
public address system, 52–53
puppets, 81

rectory, 41, 58, 66, 145, 150, 154
Regulars, 42–44
Religious Education, 13–15, 88, 98, 98–99, 103, 137
Rural Anglicanism, 42

saints, 26, 47–49
school, 13–15, 16–17, 21, 27, 48, 58–59, 67, 98–107, 119, 124
school holiday, 28
School Worship: an obituary, 14
secondary school age, 20–21, 23, 98–107
secularisation, 11, 14, 15–16
seeds, 62
servers, 44, 51
Share the Word, 54
slides, 39, 92
small congregations, 41–49
sound effects, 52–53
Stevenson, K., 50
Sunday school, 12, 13, 15–16, 17, 45, 48, 51, 57–58, 75, 126–127

Taizé, 112, 114–116, 141, 144, 151, 152
teddy bears, 79–87, 147
teenagers, 20–21, 23, 40, 45–46, 65, 68, 69, 108–116, 137–145, 147
theology, 20–21
Townwomen's Guild, 124

Understanding Christian Nurture, 19

vicarage, 41, 58, 66, 145, 150, 154
village, 59–61

wine-making, 67–68
wind, 27, 28–30, 85
Women's Institute, 34–35
woodwork, 63, 67, 69
worship committee, 126–128, 136